The short guide to town and country planning

Adam Sheppard
Nick Croft
Nick Smith

First edition published in Great Britain in 2019 by

Policy Press
University of Bristol
1-9 Old Park Hill
Bristol BS2 8BB
UK
+44 (0)117 954 5940
pp-info@bristol.ac.uk
www.policypress.co.uk

North America office:
Policy Press
c/o The University of Chicago Press
1427 East 60th Street
Chicago, IL 60637, USA
t: +1 773 702 7700
f: +1 773-702-9756
sales@press.uchicago.edu
www.press.uchicago.edu

© Policy Press 2019

British Library Cataloguing in Publication Data
A catalogue record for this book is available from the British Library.

Library of Congress Cataloging-in-Publication Data
A catalog record for this book has been requested.

ISBN 978-1-4473-4443-8 paperback
ISBN 978-1-4473-4444-5 ePub
ISBN 978-1-4473-4445-2 Mobi
ISBN 978-1-4473-4446-9 ePdf

The right of Adam Sheppard, Nick Croft and Nick Smith to be identified as the authors of this
work has been asserted by them in accordance with the Copyright, Designs and Patents Act
1988.

Cover design by Qube Design Associates, Bristol
Printed and bound in Great Britain by CMP, Poole
Policy Press uses environmentally responsible print partners

Contents

List of boxes, tables and figures

About the authors

Adam Sheppard MRTPI FRGS FHEA is a planning academic at UWE Bristol with a background from professional practice. After working as a development management planner in local government, Adam moved into academia. He now teaches and researches site scale planning implementation and decision-making.

Nick Croft MRTPI AFHEA is a senior lecturer at UWE Bristol teaching and researching local and neighbourhood planning policy and delivery. Nick joined UWE after a long and varied career in local government, where he undertook roles in policy preparation, development management, waste and minerals, and regeneration.

Nick Smith MRTPI FRGS joined UWE Bristol from planning practice where he worked in private sector consultancy on a diversity of notable projects. Nick is the Head of the Planning School at UWE Bristol, where he also teaches and researches strategic planning, infrastructure, green infrastructure and major projects.

Acknowledgements

There are many people and organisations to whom we would like to express our gratitude for their advice and encouragement in shaping the book's content.

First, our thanks to Dr Keith Lilley at Queen's University Belfast for authorisation to use his plan of Conwy Castle and town walls (as part of AHRC-funded research); the University of Texas Libraries, Austin, US, for permission to use an adaptation of the Port of Piraeus illustration; and Nick Matthews at the Town and Country Planning Association for providing the Garden City diagrams;

In addition, we would like to thank our colleagues at UWE Bristol for their support and inspiration.

Thank you also to the team at Bristol University Press, for their guidance and assistance in publishing the book.

Finally, and importantly, we would like to thank our families and friends for their love, support and assistance. The completion of this book was only possible because of you.

Thank you one and all.

Adam Sheppard, Nick Croft and Nick Smith (2018)

Preface

When we think of the governance of place, we may well think of forms of government and key actors and the manner in which their policies, plans and decisions impact upon us and where we live. Planning is central to this: town and country planning affects every element of the world we live in; every road we drive down; every street we walk along; every building, landscape and space we look at. Our experiences are shaped by the planning system in some way. This might be through a specific decision, or as a result of the provisions of legislation, but the 'universal control' provided through the planning system makes it an enormously powerful influencer on our lives. Consequently, it is important to understand the role and operation of planning in shaping and influencing our society and environment.

Despite this, our engagements with the act, art and activities of planning as a society are sometimes quite specific and limited: a neighbour planning an extension, a change of use from a shop to a takeaway, a concern over an area that is struggling economically and/or socially, a greenfield development proposal, a regeneration scheme. In some cases, it is perhaps only when we are directly and personally touched by change that we genuinely engage with planning and develop a true understanding of its scope, the way it works, the way decisions are made, and on what basis. This is understandable in many respects, but the challenge then becomes one of orientation and effective engagement by interested parties, potentially within a time-sensitive context.

For those working in planning, or in a related discipline, extensive knowledge and understanding is needed to engage effectively. This requires comprehensive training and education, whether formal or informal. Planning itself is a complex and multifaceted world, which requires professionals with a diverse and varied skills set and knowledge base to work together. This sits within a wider context of the process of development, bringing together many other professions involved in development in some way.

This book is intended to be a first step in developing your knowledge and understanding of planning. It includes a historical narrative as well as an exploration of the planning system and how it sits within professional and wider governance of place. You could be a student, home owner, neighbour, politician, community group, business person, built environment professional or simply interested in the subject; this book has been written to engage, inform and interest you.

So, whether you are beginning your studies in planning, studying a related subject at college or university which involves a need to engage with planning, working in a field linked to planning, or involved in planning or a development project yourself, it is hoped that this book will support the initial development of your knowledge and understanding. It has been designed to be either read from cover to cover, or browsed selectively, whichever context you are approaching it from. We hope you enjoy the book and find value in reading it.

Adam Sheppard, Nick Croft and Nick Smith (2018)

1

What is planning and who are the planners?

Introduction

This opening chapter provides an overview of what planning seeks to achieve and the type of outcomes that can be achieved if it is practised successfully. It presents some of the global challenges that planners are having to respond to, such as those relating to climate change, urbanisation, environmental degradation, and deteriorating health and wellbeing. The chapter presents some of the goals and principles that are being advanced for planning today, such as the need to plan for growth, and to create places that are attractive, equitable and resilient to change. Inevitably, the chapter will consider some of the tensions that can arise when planning for the 'public good'. The planning profession is also introduced, with the chapter providing some insight about the education and training of planners.

What do we mean by planning?

A dictionary definition of planning typically describes the activity of developing a proposal, or a series of proposals, for doing or achieving something. Of course, planning can relate to organising somebody's finances or a future wedding but, in the context of this book, it relates to a series of activities designed to help *manage* and *enhance* the environments in which we live, work and recreate. Both strands are equally important, and this book will discuss the type of interventions that have been, or are currently being, applied across our built and natural environments.

With respect to management, the key driver comes from the fact that land can be used for a range of possible uses. Some of these uses may be intrinsically linked to the landscape, such as a sawmill within an area of forestry. For other areas, the best or most sensible use may be less clear. For example, an area of green space on the edge of a town could be used for agriculture or recreation, but could also be used for supporting residential or commercial development.

To help manage these competing demands, somebody somewhere needs to take a decision. While influenced by political ambition, it is typically the operating planning system that seeks to offer this direction. This approach is also applicable to other scenarios, such as identifying the landscapes that need protecting and those where growth can be directed. Equally, planning systems, and the planners involved, can help to identify the most appropriate locations for things like railway stations and hospitals, or shopping destinations and schools. Very little has appeared in our environments by accident. The reality is that the shape, form and location of a development or a piece of infrastructure has been allowed and planned for a certain purpose. Some of these decisions might be visible, for instance, where development is absent from a landscape, but in other cases this influence may be subtler. For instance, planners might have intervened to ensure greater coherency in the street scene by specifying the type of building materials to be used or the heights at which building can occur.

This latter point leads on to the role of planners as enhancers, where their overall goal is to create better places. Reference to 'better' in this context is clearly open to interpretation and can have many connotations. However, planning can be used to create places that are, for example, greener, safer and more accessible. Some of these places might be new, such as where a new town or business park is being planned. However, some may be existing, for instance, where planners are seeking to improve conditions in a rundown high street or housing estate. Planners also play an important role in protecting the places that we value, such as historic buildings and coastlines, and contribute to preserving the best of our heritage.

It is likely that you will be able to identify examples of where planning has been successful. Professional bodies like the Royal Town Planning Institute (RTPI) and the American Planning Association (APA) regularly hold award events to celebrate identified successes in either plan making or site development. They also celebrate a range of places where planning has had a role to play. For example, the APA has a catalogue of 'great places', which is further broken down to identify great neighbourhoods, streets and public spaces (see APA, 2018). Equally, the RTPI has asked planners, and society in general, to identify the greatest place in Scotland (2014), England (2015), Wales (2016) and Northern Ireland (2017). The variety of places that have been nominated gives a good impression of the diverse nature of the environments in which planners find themselves working. The winner of the greatest place in England was the waterfront at Liverpool, North West England. While the location was selected for the beauty and historical significance of its environment, it was also judged to have been successful in facilitating new investment and development.

Pursuing sustainable development

The goals that planners pursue are therefore wide-ranging, but can typically be described as involving economic, environmental or social change. While certain projects can be orientated to one of these three dimensions, the core goal for planners is to ensure that their project or plan is able to deliver extensive benefits. This is central to the notion of sustainability, a concept that seeks to run through most planning systems.

The starting point for thinking sustainably is to reflect upon the 17 goals for securing sustainable development that the United Nations set in 2015 (United Nations, 2015). These are presented in Box 1.1. The goals include some ambitious targets, such as eradicating poverty, ensuring zero hunger, delivering clean water and effective sanitation, and providing affordable and clean energy. Others centre around the pursuit of economic growth, encouraging growth in innovation and infrastructure, protecting habitats and securing life on land, and acting to tackle climate change. Goal 11 seeks to make cities more inclusive, safe, resilient and sustainable. Targets for 2030 include the need to 'ensure access for all to adequate, safe and affordable housing and basic services and upgrade slums'. Over the same period, policy makers are also being pushed to 'provide universal access to safe, inclusive and accessible green and public space'. Looking across the 17 goals, it is clear that planners have an important role to play (United Nations, 2015).

Box 1.1: The United Nations Sustainable Development Goals

1. End poverty in all its forms everywhere
2. End hunger, achieve food security and improved nutrition, and promote sustainable agriculture
3. Ensure healthy lives and promote wellbeing for all at all ages
4. Ensure inclusive and equitable quality education and promote lifelong learning opportunities for all
5. Achieve gender equality and empower all women and girls
6. Ensure availability and sustainable management of water and sanitation for all
7. Ensure access to affordable, reliable, sustainable and modern energy for all
8. Promote sustained, inclusive and sustainable economic growth, full and productive employment, and decent work for all
9. Build resilient infrastructure, promote inclusive and sustainable industrialisation, and foster innovation
10. Reduce inequality within and among countries
11. Make cities and human settlements inclusive, safe, resilient and sustainable
12. Ensure sustainable consumption and production patterns

13. Take urgent action to combat climate change and its impacts (taking note of agreements made by the United Nations Framework Convention on Climate Change [UNFCCC] forum)
14. Conserve and sustainably use the oceans, seas and marine resources for sustainable development
15. Protect, restore and promote sustainable use of terrestrial ecosystems, sustainably manage forests, combat desertification and halt and reverse land degradation, and halt biodiversity loss
16. Promote peaceful and inclusive societies for sustainable development, provide access to justice for all and build effective, accountable and inclusive institutions at all levels
17. Strengthen the means of implementation and revitalise the global partnership for sustainable development

Source: United Nations (2015)

Planning at a range of spatial scales

Although these goals have universal relevance, planning as an activity occurs at a range of spatial scales. Specifically, planning can occur with respect to an individual building or space, a street, a neighbourhood, a whole town or city, or a town and city and its surrounding rural hinterland. Planning activity can also expand at scales beyond to encompass plans for regions, whole countries or global regions.

Planners therefore look at the big picture. So, while architects will tend to start by looking at an individual building, the planner looks at the wider area to determine its broader needs, before identifying the type of parameters and principles that would be best applied to an individual site. Planners are mindful about how the different parts of a community fit together, as if they are creating some kind of jigsaw puzzle.

Irrespective of the scale, the processes for creating a plan, and the policies and proposals that they entail, tend to be similar. Greater detail will be provided in Chapter 4, but the starting point rests with identifying the challenges affecting the area.

Planning challenges

The challenges that planners need to respond to are diverse and it is difficult to provide full coverage here. Three of the most significant are presented below.

Responding to changing growth

Understanding the changing nature of growth, in either a positive or negative sense, tends to be a core driver in the planning of space. Most places across the world are growing, with global projections showing how the world's population will grow (from 7.6 billion now) to 8.6 billion in 2030, 9.8 billion in 2050 and 11.2 billion in 2100 (United Nations, 2017). While growth rates vary, the significance of this trend is amplified by the projection that 60% of the world's population will live in urban areas by 2030 (United Nations, 2017). Furthermore, 95% of the urban expansion expected in future decades is to be in the developing world. Not only does this present a challenge for possible overcrowding, and place additional strain on urban infrastructure, it also leads to questions around where new growth should be directed. In these locations, planners need to ensure development is directed to the right place, with residents expecting to have access to jobs, healthcare, education and other forms of infrastructure. Equally, planners need to ensure that the locations chosen for development are not physically or environmentally constrained, and developers do not use locations that would impact upon a certain habitat or species. Care also needs to be directed to the form, design and energy efficiency of new development. As the United Nations has recently explained, while the world's cities occupy just 3% of the earth's land surface, they account for 60–80% of energy consumption and 75% of carbon emissions (United Nations, 2015).

Linked to these concerns over supply, planners also need to be mindful about the affordability of available property and the ability of homes to meet different housing demands. For example, planners are challenged to deliver homes of different sizes and types, and to ensure that homes are inclusive and adaptive to change as the needs of their occupiers shift over time.

The UK is experiencing more moderate rates of growth, but its population is still projected to increase by 3.6 million (5.5%) over the next 10 years, from an estimated 65.6 million in mid-2016 to 69.2 million in mid-2026 (Office for National Statistics, 2018). Equally, while the capacity to accommodate this growth may be higher than in developing world areas, there is still significant challenge with accommodating, for example, the 300,000 homes that need to be supplied in England each year (at least according to the government). One of the challenges is delivering the number of homes felt to be needed, with recent housing supply figures for England extending from around 124,720 (2012/13) to approximately 217,350 (2016/17) (Wilson et al, 2018). The other challenge, which will be discussed later, surrounds public acceptability, with ongoing questions being raised about the number of homes felt to be necessary and the best place for accommodating them.

While most places are experiencing growth, there are others that are experiencing population loss and decline. One of the most documented is the city of Detroit in the United States, which has seen a decline in population of 61.4% between 1950 and 2010 (Business Insider, 2013). Elsewhere, population loss has been more recent, with cities such as Makeyevka (Ukraine) and Khulna (Bangladesh) experiencing decline of 11.3% and 13.6% respectively between 2005 and 2015 (*Financial Times*, 2017).

Planners therefore need to think about the places that are becoming depopulated, perhaps as a result of populations being drawn to cities and other urban areas. A dwindling population could adversely impact on service provision, thereby affecting the ability of residents to access schools, transport and shopping facilities.

Responding to a changing climate

Another key challenge that planners are having to respond to is human-induced climate change. As the Intergovernmental Panel on Climate Change (IPCC) has said, temperature rises could be in the order of between 2.5 and 10 degrees Fahrenheit over the next century. Impacts are likely to vary with time but are likely to include changes to precipitation patterns, more droughts and heatwaves, and the expansion of seawater and melting land ice leading to an increase in sea levels. Sea levels have already risen by 8 inches (203 mm) since records began in 1880 but are projected to increase by a further 1–4 feet (0.3–1.2 m) by 2100 (IPCC, 2014). While the impacts will be universal, their size and magnitude are likely to vary with the ability of different locations to apply appropriate adaptation and mitigation. In this context, adaptation means taking appropriate action to prevent or minimise the damage that climate change can cause, or taking advantage of the opportunities that a warmer climate could give rise to. Mitigation, on the other hand, refers to efforts to reduce or prevent emissions of greenhouse gases. Planners clearly have responsibilities in both areas, as evidenced through the various plans and strategies that have been developed in response to climate change at a range of spatial scales. These include a number of actions and goals, from helping to facilitate the delivery of renewable energy, to limiting the carbon emissions arising from built development. Planners are also involved in developing solutions to the likely consequences of climate change, such as providing new flood defences.

Improving health and wellbeing

In addition to responding to changing levels of population growth, planners also have an important role in ensuring that the health and wellbeing of society is maintained and enhanced as fully as possible. This is a wide-ranging challenge and includes endeavours for delivering safe access to water, providing appropriate sanitation and ensuring access to clean air. For this latter challenge, the World

Health Organization (WHO) attributed outdoor air pollution to causing 3 million premature deaths worldwide in 2012. A further 4.3 million deaths were caused by indoor air pollution: exposure to toxic smoke from burning solid fuels such as wood and coal is a particularly significant problem in Asia and Africa. The WHO claims that 92% of the world's population lives in places where air pollution exceeds WHO guideline limits (WHO, 2018a).

Obesity represents another major problem. The WHO states that obesity has nearly tripled since 1975, with 1.9 billion adults (aged 18+) being overweight in 2016, and 650 million of these being obese. In that same year, 41 million children under the age of 5 were overweight or obese (WHO, 2018b).

While a range of factors lie behind worsening air quality and obesity, planners have a role to play. For instance, in relation to air quality in towns and cities, planners can play a part by trying to reduce road congestion, encouraging a shift to public transport and promoting active forms of movement, such as walking and cycling. Planting trees and providing green space can also make a difference. Active forms of transport can also help to tackle growing weight levels, while planners can also act by safeguarding and providing sports facilities to encourage sport and recreation. Providing necessary facilities close to homes and businesses is also an important goal if travel is to be minimised, while protecting and planning for allotments and community gardens can help to encourage communities to eat healthily. These interventions can play an important role in improving physical health, but planners can also play a part in enhancing mental health as well. For instance, providing spaces such as community centres and libraries can help to encourage social interaction and lessen the risk of social isolation and depression (Barton, 2016).

Planning across a range of timescales

Although planners look to respond to current challenges, they are also mindful of the need to look ahead. In doing so, they need to consider the type of changes that are likely to affect the built and natural environments which they are responsible for. As such, they need to be aware of relevant trends and projections, and the possible scenarios that could arise in response. Some of these seem quite certain, with computer modelling being used to create the type of growth projections mentioned above. However, the reality is that nobody truly knows how a trend or projection will manifest itself. Planners can either ignore these future scenarios and only plan for the short term or take an educated guess by using the best information available to them. This tends to be the route taken. Planners do need to think long-term, as the actions that are likely to be necessary will be complex and will require a clear strategy in order for them to become a reality. For example, planning to accommodate increased housing demand through constructing a new community or creating a new rail link is not something that can be done hastily. It is for this reason that planners tend to use timescales that extend across 10, 15 or 20 years.

This emphasis is difficult for some to comprehend, with society generally feeling more confident in responding to something more tangible (like plans for a new house to be developed in the next year) than an idea that is more conceptual (like plans for the siting of a new airport that could happen in the next 20 years). Clearly, looking to the future is also not an easy thing to do. Can we really predict what our lives will be like in 20 years' time? The reality is that the way we live, or the ways in which we work, shop or recreate, might be very different to the ways that we do these things now. This is usefully illustrated by thinking back 10 years. While certain things are likely to have remained the same, other aspects of daily life will have changed a lot, particularly with respect to those elements where technology plays a part. For example, it is questionable whether commentators, including planners, saw the potential for online banking and the gradual decline of the high-street bank (despite the impact that their demise has had on the high street). Planners therefore need to consider the impact of future technologies, such as delivery drones or autonomous vehicles, as fully as possible.

Other challenges

Apart from the subject and technical challenges that planners must endure day to day, barriers can also arise in response to political challenge or influence. As you will see in subsequent chapters, many decisions relating to planning are dependent on decisions taken by those who have been elected into power. While their impact may be direct, such as where they have been placed into power on an anti-development stance, their influence might be subtler, for instance, where they can contribute to discussions over plan direction or on agreeing the level of finance for the planning service. The public, and other key stakeholders, can also have a significant influence, particularly where they are sceptical about a vision or are in straight opposition to a scheme that, on paper, has the potential to deliver multiple benefits.

Planning as a profession

Planning as an activity has a long-established history, with attempts to manage and create space dating back to early civilisation. People have therefore been practising planning for centuries but planning, as a professional activity, has a more recent history. Indeed, planners, as a distinct group of professionals, have only been in existence since the early 1900s. An early driver in the promotion of debates concerning place, and the type of communities we should be creating, came from the work of Sir Ebenezer Howard, who presented the notion of a garden city via his 1898 book, *To-Morrow: A Peaceful Path to Real Reform* (Hall and Tewdwr-Jones, 2010). While this concept is described at a later stage in the book, Howard also founded the Garden Cities Association that enabled a mixing of views around the themes of design, health and wellbeing, social justice and economic efficiency. The composition of the group was mixed, with no one particular group or profession dominating. The association still exists but is now known as the Town and Country Planning Association (TCPA, 2018). Interestingly, Howard was also the first president of the International Garden Cities and Town Planning Association, which was inaugurated in 1913. This association also remains in place today under the name of the International Federation for Housing and Planning.

The term 'town planning' was first used in Britain in 1906. The first piece of planning legislation was the Housing, Town Planning, etc Act of 1909. As Chapter 2 will explain, this allowed local planning authorities to create schemes for parcels of land being redeveloped. The schemes were particularly useful for the urban fringe, where the plans helped to define a layout and provide prescription over density (Hall and Tewdwr-Jones, 2010). Those producing the schemes were representative of several different professions, but came mainly from the disciplines of engineering, surveying, architecture and law. The emergence of a planning profession developed following the appointment of one of these early practitioners, Thomas Adams, as a Town Planning Inspector at the Local Government Board. As Thomas began to regularly meet those preparing the schemes, a community of practice soon developed which ultimately led to the creation of a Town Planning Institute in the UK in 1914.

The institute received a Royal Charter in 1959 and took on the name of the Royal Town Planning Institute (RTPI).

The RTPI today

In January 2018 the institute had over 25,150 members. The majority of these are based in the UK, although the RTPI reports that it has 1,420 international members in over 82 countries. Approximately 60% of members are men, but the RTPI, and other institutes worldwide, are actively engaged in ensuring that the profession is as diverse as the communities that planners seek to serve (RTPI, 2018). The RTPI is a charity as well as a learned society. It is responsible for maintaining professional standards and does this by accrediting university courses and assessing the professional competence of eligible students wishing to join the profession. It also sets out requirements for lifelong learning and obliges members to accord with a professional code of conduct (the basics of which will be considered later). As a learned society, the RTPI seeks to advance the art and science of planning for the benefit of the public and actively lobbies the government, and other relevant bodies, about the value of planning.

Worldwide planning institutes

The RTPI's website includes the details of other international groups that represent global planners. Over 80 are listed, with all continents being represented. Examples include the Urban Planning Society of China (1956), the Institute of Town Planners, India (1947), the Planning Institute of Australia (1951) and the Nigerian Institute of Town Planners (1968). The American Planning Association is the largest and has 38,000 members. It dates its history to 1917 when planners came together to form the American City Planning Institute.

There is some effective engagement between these institutes, although collaboration is also encouraged through a range of other networks. These include the Commonwealth Association of Planners (CAP), which has 40,000 members in over 27 countries, and the International Society of City and Regional Planners (ISOCARP), which was founded in 1965 to bring planners together to share challenges and best practice. The European Council of Spatial Planners/Conseil Européen des Urbanistes was formed in 1985 and brings together 25 professional spatial planning associations and institutes from 23 European countries, as well as corresponding members. The council hosts working groups, has a biannual awards scheme, and arranges a wide range of conferences and events.

Practising planning

Irrespective of where they are based, the challenges facing most planners are likely to be quite similar. While their professional training will guide them to certain solutions, their exact response will ultimately depend on the legislation, policy and organisational structure of the country in which they are working. The type of organisation they will find themselves working for will also vary.

According to the RTPI, approximately 60% of its members work in the public sector. A further 33% work in the private sector, with 7% being employed across the voluntary sector (RTPI, 2018).

Working in the public sector

Roles within the public sector will become clearer as you progress through this book but, in a UK sense, will involve working at a local planning authority. These are distributed across the country but the size of each organisation, and the workload it supports, inevitably varies. However, most will be employed either in the making and implementation of policy and plans or in the assessment of site development proposals via the application of development management.

Those working in development management will be involved in discussing potential projects with applicants, reviewing planning applications once received, seeking comment from relevant stakeholders (including the public), and coming to a decision about whether the project should be approved or refused. If it is approved, the planner will need to release a final list of planning conditions and confirm the details of any legal agreement (as discussed later). If the project is refused, the planner will be expected to explain the reasoning for their decision via a formal decision notice and prepare for a potential resubmission of the scheme. As noted later, they might also need to participate in defending their decision via any planning appeal lodged by the applicant. Planners engaged in this type of work are essentially acting on behalf of their authority employer, as well as the local politicians (the councillors) who have been elected to represent their constituents. Having good knowledge of planning law and policy is essential for such a role, as is the ability to demonstrate good customer service to the wide range of people that development management staff will meet.

Linked to development management is enforcement: a dedicated team of staff who are responsible for ensuring that policy is adhered to and for helping to oversee the delivery of consented schemes as intended.

Policy roles are perhaps more diverse. Staff in these teams will be responsible for setting policies, developing proposals, and imposing certain constraints and controls across environments deemed to be particularly significant. In addition to advising the public, as well as developers and other groups, about the implications of policy on a certain piece of land, they will be charged with creating a plan for the area. As we will see in Chapter 4, this is a multistage process that can take a number of years from start to finish.

Planners working on such a plan will need to collect relevant evidence, analyse this to help define relevant area challenges, and use these prompts to develop the policy context of the plan. Despite the differences in geography, plans tend to have a similar composition, beginning with the setting of a vision and continuing with the development of relevant aims and objectives. They will assess the merit of pursuing different policy goals, by applying a sustainability appraisal, and develop a set of policies and proposals. Some of the policies will be positive in their wording while others will be more constraining, for instance, in telling a developer that they will only be able to pursue their scheme if certain conditions are met. Plans are typically ordered by theme, with policy being prepared for such things as employment, retailing and green space. A monitoring framework to assess the performance of the plan is also normally included. Apart from developing the plan, and keeping it reviewed and up to date, policy planners might also be involved in preparing site-specific guidance (typically known as a development brief), or some more detailed (and supplementary) policy on topics that might include conservation, design or car parking standards. Working to maintain, or develop, a plan's evidence base will require planners to consult such things as population or household forecasts, and to undertake or commission research into areas of change or concern.

Working in the private sector

Planners working in the private sector will be based at broader range of organisations. Some will be employed as a planner within a more general organisation, such as a retailer, a transport provider or a house-builder. Their work will be centred around what their organisation is looking to achieve, but is likely to revolve around the securing of planning permission or contributing to the shaping of a local development plan to ensure it meets their employer's needs. For some organisations, having a planner within their team might be a luxury, particularly if their engagement with the planning system is limited or sporadic. Under these circumstances, an organisation might choose to appoint a planning consultancy to act on their behalf. This sector has grown significantly in the UK over the last 30 years, with a range of companies now in place. These consultancies vary in their size and the services that they offer. Some will choose to work in certain geographical areas while others will prefer to work with a certain type of development (such as energy or housing). Others will be multidisciplinary in their composition, with planning potentially being combined with services in architecture, urban design or environmental consultancy. The largest companies often have a focus on engineering, and some of these operate internationally. Most planning consultancies in the UK tend to have multiple office locations, with the majority of these tending to be city-based.

Planners working for a private consultancy are likely to have a mixed portfolio of work, and to work with a range of projects and clients at any one time. Work is completed to an agreed fee, with planners having to compete to secure an appropriate supply of work. As a result, planners working in the private sector are expected to demonstrate the same customer service skills as their public-sector colleagues, but largely for the purposes of ensuring that their clients remain faithful and return to them with future work.

A search on the internet should generate some examples of a typical planning consultancy. The RTPI also offers an online directory where consultancies can be searched based on geography and specialism. Example practices include Arup, Atkins, Barton Willmore, David Lock Associates, DLP, LUC, Pegasus and Terence O'Rourke.

Studying to become a planner

Planning is not a topic that is typically taught at school, but it does permeate the curricula of several subjects, including geography, economics, politics, psychology and design technology. To satisfy the educational requirements of the RTPI, it is necessary to follow an accredited programme of study. This can either be via an undergraduate programme or via a postgraduate programme following a cognate degree. Some students also opt to study planning while working in the sector via a technical or degree apprenticeship. Perhaps confusingly, the names of planning courses tend to vary, with the terms 'urban planning', 'town planning', 'town and country planning' and 'city and regional planning' being used interchangeably. However, the content of each course tends to be broadly similar. It is also common for planning to be combined with other aligned subjects, such as architecture, geography and property development. To access these accredited programmes, students need to study at approved and 'effective' planning schools.

Once an accredited programme has been successfully completed, a student can progress to become a chartered member of the institute. There are two principal routes for doing this. The most common includes following the RTPI's Assessment of Professional Competence, which requires the candidate to undertake two years of professional experience that will coincide with the student's first job (extended periods of work experience undertaken during a student's degree can reduce this post-degree requirement to a year if certain conditions are met). During this time, candidates or licentiates must reflect upon their experiences and the learning achieved from them.

To formally apply for chartered membership, licentiates must submit statements outlining their professional experience and the professional competencies that they have developed and applied through their work. They also need to supply a professional development plan. If their application is successful, licentiates are formally elected to become chartered members of the RTPI. This means that they can use the letters 'MRTPI' after their name. An alternative, but longer, route to chartered membership involves replacing part of the study requirements of the RTPI with additional experience. By taking this route, licentiates progress to become associate members before converting to become full chartered members of the RTPI. Members of the RTPI are obliged to adhere to a professional code of conduct and pursue a set amount of study for the purposes of supporting their continuing and professional development. A range of events and resources are provided by the RTPI to support this learning, and you might be interested in attending one of these yourself. Details can be found by searching 'RTPI events' on the internet.

As you would expect, accredited programmes provide the knowledge, as well as the practical and personal skills, that practising planners are expected to need. The RTPI's *Policy Statement on Initial Planning Education* (RTPI, 2012) provides an important set of expectations that planning schools are expected to meet. Similarly, the *Subject benchmark statement for town and country planning*, as produced by the Quality Assurance Agency for Higher Education, provides some useful prompts concerning the type of knowledge and understanding that planning graduates are expected to show (QAA, 2016). These knowledge areas seek to ensure graduates understand the 'causes and processes of change in the environment', and to ensure students understand the 'practice of planning' and contemporary 'debates in planning'. The first heading emphasises the need for graduates to consider such things as the processes of socioeconomic and political change and their spatial outcomes, as well as development processes, development economics, and the nature of land and property markets. Similarly, the statement directs students to understand the processes of environmental, ecological and physical change, and the associated threats from climate change and natural or human-made disasters. Understanding the need for climate adaptation and mitigation is also outlined as a priority, as is the need to understand interactions in and between the built and natural environments. Expected areas of knowledge relating to 'planning practice' are outlined in Box 1.2 below.

Box 1.2: Expected areas of knowledge and understanding relating to planning practice

- Impacts and consequences of planning upon individuals, communities and key interest groups
- Political and institutional frameworks at all levels, and their procedures
- Legal, regulatory and governance arrangements for planning
- The planning and delivery of housing
- Plan and policy-making methods, techniques and processes at a variety of scales
- Participation and working with diverse communities
- Planning as a tool for delivering sustainable and inclusive development
- Awareness, understanding and practice of design, including aesthetic and inclusive design issues
- Application of knowledge to action, and theory to practice
- The practice of planning in a variety of international, institutional, professional, legal and cultural settings
- Administrative and management arrangements for effective planning
- Management, financing and implementation of planning projects
- Interdisciplinary and multidisciplinary working and problem solving
- Standards of ethical practice
- Infrastructure (including transport) planning and delivery

Source: Quality Assurance Agency for Higher Education (2016: 9)

Over the years, a considerable amount of work has been undertaken to help unpack the skills that planners need day to day. A good and fairly recent example is the *National Competency Framework for Planners* that was jointly prepared by the RTPI and the Planning Advisory

Service (2013). A selection of key competencies are outlined in Box 1.3.

Box 1.3: Key competencies for planning

Creative vision

- Producing creative and innovative strategies and solutions
- Making lateral connections
- Aesthetic and design awareness and critique

Project management

- Defining objectives
- Delivering – making it happen given constraints
- Resource management, including financial and personnel management and use of information technology
- Process management and evaluation

Problem solving

- Problem definition
- Data collection, investigation and research
- Quantitative and qualitative analysis and appraisal
- Weighing evidence and evaluation of alternative solutions
- Decision-making

Leadership

- Inspiring and motivating others at all levels
- Leading by example – displaying enthusiasm, tenacity, flexibility and self-motivation
- Embracing and leading through change
- People and organisational management
- Coaching and mentoring

Collaborative and multidisciplinary working

- Partnership working – engaging with all professionals employed in the creation of sustainable communities and the built environment

- Creating an environment where information is shared
- Effective networking

Communication
- Written, oral, graphic and multimedia communication
- Listening actively
- Using appropriate communication methods tailored to the audience
- Managing misinformation
- Internal communication and information sharing
- Community involvement and facilitation

Source: RTPI and PAS (2013)

Conclusion

This opening chapter has introduced the kind of themes and challenges that planners engage with. It has outlined some of the features that underpin planning, such as the need to plan for the long term, and the kind of places where planners work. As part of this, the chapter has introduced planning as a professional activity. It has also summarised the ways in which people can become professional and chartered members and the type of skills and knowledge that they will be expected to have.

Further reading

For a more detailed consideration of the matters discussed in this chapter, the following texts are recommended:

Barton, H. (2016) *City of well-being: A radical guide to planning*, London: Routledge.

Clifford, B. and Tewdwr-Jones, M. (2013) *The collaborating planner? Practitioners in the neoliberal age*, Bristol: Policy Press.

Couch, C. (2016) *Urban planning: An introduction*, Basingstoke: Palgrave.

Greed, C. and Johnson, D. (2014) *Planning in the UK: An introduction*, London: Palgrave Macmillan.

Rydin, Y. (2011) *The purpose of planning: Creating sustainable towns and cities*, Bristol: Policy Press.

Websites

Useful websites include:

American Planning Association: https://www.planning.org

China Association of City Planning: www.cacp.org.cn

Commonwealth Association of Planners: https://www.commonwealth-planners.org

European Council of Spatial Planners/Conseil Européen des Urbanistes: www.ectp-ceu.eu/index.php/en

Institute of Town Planners, India: www.itpi.org.in

International Association for China Planning: www.chinaplanning.org/alpha

International Federation for Housing and Planning: www.ifhp.org

International Society of City and Regional Planners: https://isocarp.org

Nigerian Institute of Town Planners: http://nitpng.com

Planning Institute of Australia: https://www.planning.org.au

Royal Town Planning Institute: www.rtpi.org.uk

Town and Country Planning Association: www.tcpa.org.uk

2

Pre-war history

Introduction

> The greater the insight gained into ideas, inspirations, success
> and failures of predecessors in town planning and building, the
> greater will be the understanding of qualities of environment that
> enable people as a community to enjoy a healthy and agreeable
> life. (Burke, 1975: 3)

This chapter explores how humans have sought to organise the
built and natural environment since ancient times. We highlight
some of the main factors that have influenced the urban form of our
21st-century towns and cities in the United Kingdom. In doing so,
we look at how previous approaches to planning can help us interpret
its contribution towards our present-day needs, as well as how we
can make appropriate changes for the future, and hopefully avoid
mistakes of the past. We then focus our attention on how planning
has changed in the 'modern' post-1947 era up to the present day.

Planning in the ancient and classical world

People have consciously planned their environment to a greater or
lesser extent ever since acquiring the necessary understanding and
ability to offer choice in where to live (Burke, 1975: 5). The transition
from living in naturally occurring caves to constructing purpose-
built shelters, and then from socialising as small family groups to

larger communities, heralded a change from mere subsistence to one in which there could be an organised division of labour, thus sustaining a higher standard of living.

Sumerian cities began to develop around 3500 BC and are generally acknowledged as the 'cradle of urban civilisation' (Burke, 1975: 7). Walled defensive structures encircled dwellings, workplaces and public buildings, and were administered by a hierarchy of religious and secular bureaucrats. A similar Bronze Age civilisation was occurring in the Punjab area of the Indus during the period 3250 to 1700 BC. One of the first known and understood examples of a human settlement having been 'planned' is at Kahun, Egypt (Aldridge, 1915: 11). Built as a place to house the construction workers of the pyramid of Illahun, it dates from about 2650 BC (Burke, 1975: 8) and incorporates the earliest known example of drainage channels along the streets (Petrie, 2013). And around 2000 BC, the Minoan civilisation on Crete, situated on a strategic route between Europe and Egypt in the Mediterranean, was flourishing with elaborate palaces, public buildings and sophisticated sanitation arrangements. Britain, by comparison, at that time had 'sparse and primitive' communal living (Burke, 1975: 11).

The first known 'town planner' is attributed by the ancient Greek philosopher Aristotle (Aldridge, 1915: 14) as being Hippodamus of Miletus (born around 480 BC). He is best known for laying out the port of Athens (Piraeus) in 450 BC using straight and intersecting streets with grouped housing and a balanced distribution of public and residential uses (Aldridge, 1915: 14; Abercrombie, 1933: 32; Burke, 1975: 19) (see Figure 2.1). There are many important attributes when selecting a site for a settlement, including the presence of a ready supply of water, a navigational trade route with opportunities for taxing crossing points, and defensive potential (such as higher ground and naturally occurring physical barriers). But in addition to these Aristotle identified 'health' as being the most important characteristic of planning an ideal city, a theme we shall return to later.

The potential for a settlement to serve as a centre for local governance and religious worship was also of importance. To

Figure 2.1: Port of Piraeus 480 BC, showing the grid layout of the building blocks

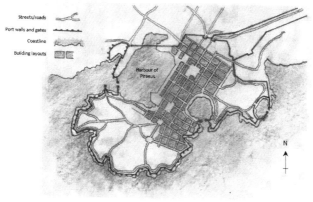

Adapted from a drawing by Walther Judeich (1905), courtesy of the University of Texas Libraries, the University of Texas, Austin.

facilitate such activities, settlements would often have a centrally located open space for meetings and markets – referred to as *agora* in Greek and *forum* in Roman – adjacent to which were administrative and religious buildings. Once sited, cities would subsequently often grow incrementally. In doing so they became overcrowded and unhealthy, such that by the time there was sufficient wealth and organisation within a city to effect beneficial change, the street patterns and uses of land were so intermingled that retrofitting measures for sanitation was problematical and largely disregarded.

By Roman times,[1] the two main factors that impacted on the use of predetermined town planning principles were the need to house a rapidly expanding population, and problematic site topography and ground conditions (Burke, 1975: 29), which are similar issues to those we still face today. In Rome itself there was no overarching plan for development, with little of the 'utilitarian regularity' (Abercrombie, 1933: 42) often associated with Roman settlements. The ad hoc development of Rome sits in stark contrast to the geometrically planned garrison towns in the conquered territories such as Britain. Roman garrison towns were typically laid out on a grid street pattern forming *insulae*, square plots or blocks of land for building, usually occupied by between one and four houses or public buildings (Abercrombie, 1933: 40). Towns were surrounded by rectangular defensive walls pierced on each side by a gate whose streets converged at a forum in the centre (see Figure 2.2), usually incorporating drainage and piped water.

The Romans occupied Britain (Britannia) from AD 43 until AD 410, during which time both town and countryside prospered.

The regional imprint made by cleared forests, drained marshes, deep-ploughed fields, worked mines and industrial activity, by the location of ports, regional capitals, market towns and of London itself, and, above all, by the skilfully routed highways,

Figure 2.2: Roman Gloucester (indicative layout)

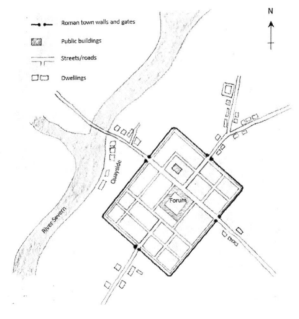

was firm enough to be decipherable and in part renewed centuries later. The urban imprint of orderly and logical street patters, well-laid water supply and sewer pipes, stone building foundations, walled fortifications and town gates, was not lightly erased: and it occasionally survived to determine, and even dominate, the layout of some twentieth-century towns. (Burke, 1975: 40)

The Dark Ages

The withdrawal of Roman forces from Britain in the 5th century left a framework of buildings and supporting infrastructure that can still be identified today. However, Britain became a place divided among a number of rulers. This was compounded by Viking raids in the north and east, requiring the primary function of settlements to revert from shelter and subsistence back to defence.

In 871 Alfred became King of Wessex, the largest remaining kingdom in the southern and western parts of the land that was to eventually become known as England. He adopted a strategic approach to locating walled settlements, called *burhs*, within 20 miles (32 km) of each other (a day's march for his warriors). Critical to this purpose was a network of routes, known as *herepaths*, connecting the burhs so that they could defend and reinforce each other in the face of Viking attacks. Across Wessex, 33 burhs of varying sizes were constructed, some, such as Winchester, were on sites of former Roman settlements, meaning that existing defensive walls could be reused, although internal street layouts were extensively re-planned (Biddle and Hill, 1971). In other places new structures were required, such as wide ditches, earth mounds and palisades. Similarly, the invading Vikings constructed their own military settlements, which they called *boroughs* – a word still used today, unlike the Wessex equivalent.

The term 'Dark Ages' is commonly used as an alternative to the 'Early Middle Ages', and references the relative decline post Roman occupation up until the Norman Conquest in 1066. The term can be considered misleading in some respects, though, with a diversity of changes occurring during this period. However, with attention largely focused on settlement fortification progress, it is true that, in town planning terms, progress was somewhat limited during this period and, at least on that basis, it could appropriately be referred to as the Dark Ages to a certain extent. Despite this, the combined network of *burhs* and *boroughs* with connecting routeways lent itself to effective local governance and with it trade flourished. Indeed, many settlements have continued to function through the centuries and now comprise present-day market towns forming important administrative centres (Burke, 1975: 45). The systems of governance that emerged during this period, together with the manner in which this governance influenced the built environment, are therefore important to the history of the planning system in the UK.

Planning in medieval times

Europe in the medieval period operated under a feudal system of governance.[2] A hierarchy of relationships dictated how countries functioned: at the top, politically and militarily, all the way down to peasants' day-to-day subsistence. Such centralised control was imposed in Britain after the Norman conquest of 1066. Growth in international trade in the centuries that followed contributed to the wealth of towns and led to the construction of many new town boroughs. In the 40 years 1191–1230 some 49 new towns were established, referred to as being 'planted', most of which were adjacent to a castle controlled by the Crown (Beresford, 1967: 327). Despite this, much of medieval Britain was rural in character, with people living in dispersed settlements close to their places of work. Towns did not support large populations; for example, York, a regionally important settlement, had around eight thousand inhabitants, whereas county towns such as Warwick, Gloucester and Leicester had around three to four thousand people. Only London, the country's capital was on a different scale with a population of approximately fifty thousand in late medieval times (Platt, 1976: 15).

There were generally two types of medieval town: those that were planned as a coherent whole at a particular point in time (for example,

Conwy, North Wales, constructed 1283, see Figure 2.3), and, more commonly, those that grew up organically over time, usually on or at the joining of trade routes, although even these normally had their origins in pre-existing settlements. The former were often rectangular in shape, or as close as possible given topographic limitations, whereas the latter generally fanned out from defensive walls as 'ribbon development' along trading paths. However, even a planned town, once established, would then grow organically as the need for expansion arose (Hindle, 2002: 8).

Medieval town planning largely concerned 'selecting and acquiring a site, ensuring a water supply, deciding on the alignment of walls/fortifications/gates, subdivision into plots for buildings, identifying a location for the market and church' (Burke, 1975: 47). Such planning, however, was undertaken for the benefit of the present, with little consideration given to how the place might need to expand as the population and trading/manufacturing increased.

Figure 2.3: Medieval walled town of Conwy, North Wales, circa 1300

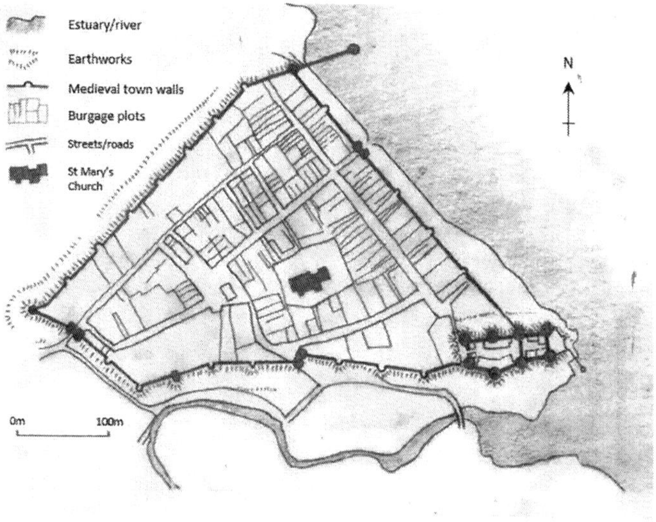

Based on a plan by Lilley et al (2005).

Trade was central to the successful operation of the medieval town. In 1298 King Edward I called upon specialist 'planners' to advise on 'how to divide, order and arrange a new town in the manner that will be most beneficial to us and the merchants' (Inigo Triggs, 1911; Beresford, 1967: 3–13). It was in the public interest to protect this function both within its walls and by enabling trade between towns, for example, through the construction and maintenance of roads, bridges, waterways and wharfs.

A town's main trading occurred in the marketplace, which was normally at its centre. The shape of marketplaces in some towns, for example, Nottingham and Hereford, are triangular due to the converging of three major trading routes. Others, for example, Pembroke in west Wales, are rectangular where the road widens to facilitate the sale of goods from individual *burgage plots*. These plots were generally narrow-fronted onto the street, but with extended land to the rear at a ratio of around 1:6 (Platt, 1976: 30). This allowed the maximum number of traders to front onto the main streets for selling their goods, with backland given over to the growing of fruit and vegetables. It also meant that, despite popular misconceptions, towns in the Middle Ages were generally not cramped, with densities of only around 15–20 dwellings per acre not uncommon (including curtilage and access paths) (Burke, 1975: 63). It was in the post-medieval period that pressure to build on backland areas within the town walls resulted in significantly increased densities. Some burgage plots are indicated on the Conwy plan (see Figure 2.3).

Early medieval towns did not have identifiable residential and commercial zones, due to shop/business owners living in rooms above their premises, although administrative public buildings tended to occupy central locations. The specialisation of certain trades in particular parts of the town was driven by specific practical necessities such as the need for large quantities of fresh running water (Platt, 1976: 47). Businesses with more unpleasant odours and impacts, such as butchers, fishmongers and tanneries, were on a relatively small scale and, given the primary importance of ensuring one's livelihood, meant that initially such inconveniences were tolerated. Towards the later Middle Ages, as the intensity and volume increased, these enterprises were 'assigned specific localities where their activities could do least harm' (Platt, 1976: 47), which implies a degree of zonal planning being undertaken by those governing the settlement.

In the 13th century sanitation and health were becoming of greater importance for town authorities, who would use taxes to suitably surface their streets such that the accumulation of noxious matter was easier to remove and streets were easier to traverse (Platt, 1976: 49, 69). At the time, many town houses had their own toilet, known as a garderobe: essentially a stone-lined pit in the cellar that was emptied at regular intervals, normally at night due to the smell. By the later Middle Ages there were public latrines and piped fresh water in many towns (Platt, 1976: 69).

There was significant economic disparity in medieval times between those living within and those outside of a town's gated walls. As the rule of law increased and the threat of invasion diminished, the symbolic enclosure of wealth and prosperity from the surrounding rurality of the countryside's peasantry became more important than defensive fortification (Platt, 1976). In contrast to towns, the countryside changed relatively little until the late 14th century. The feudal system that tied a worker to his lord's manor was effectively ended by a combination of labour shortages, caused by the Black Death in 1348–49, and then the Peasants' Revolt of 1381, which allowed peasants to sell their labour to the highest bidder. The reduction in population following the Black Death, by around forty per cent, resulted in a stagnating economy which did not pick up again until the Tudor period in the sixteenth century (Hindle, 2002: 9).

It merits highlighting that during this period we can identify some of the earliest forms of regulatory control for the built environment in the UK, and specifically in London. This was emerging through the structure of governance in place and is perhaps best compared to the Building Regulations of the modern day, but it is important because it demonstrates a form of state intervention into the built environment. The most notable piece to highlight perhaps is the Assize of Nuisance. As noted by Sheppard et al:

A part of the Assize Courts system in place at that time, the Assize of Nuisance represented a set of regulations concerning property rights and the management of nuisance in relation to property and its use. (Sheppard et al, 2017: 43)

The system we see emerging at this time was limited in scope, geography and application, but it was nevertheless a key early step in the developments that were witnessed during this period.

Renaissance and Tudor planning

The Renaissance covers the period from approximately the 14th to the 18th centuries and is often referred to as a 'bridging period' between the medieval and modern worlds. Deriving from the northern shores of the Mediterranean, ideas on how to create the 'ideal city' abounded at this time. 'It was in the first place definitely architectural in character, aiming at magnificence of design in place of the more military, utilitarian and colonial objects of Roman and Medieval' (Abercrombie, 1933: 53). Hall and Tewdwr-Jones refer to the Baroque era of the 17th and 18th centuries as 'the greatest flowering of formal town planning before the Industrial Revolution' (2010: 12).

The planning of urban settlements during the Renaissance on the European mainland was often an expression of regal or papal power (Hall and Tewdwr-Jones, 2010: 12) and took on an artistic merit such that the towns looked impressive on paper, often incorporating striking geometric shapes and features radiating from a central focal point. However, in seeking artistic symmetry and perfection, there was a failure to appreciate that a town's population changes, as do the needs of its economy, which does not sit easily within a fixed geometric configuration. 'The cardinal fault in ideal-city planning was the attempt to contain within a static and rigid physical structure something that is neither static nor rigid but dynamic and fluctuating' (Burke, 1975: 78).

Box 2.1: The five principles of Renaissance planning in Europe

Abercrombie (1933: 57) notes that Renaissance planning on the continent was chiefly influenced by five principles:

1. The primary straight street: a method taken from Roman design to provide an 'avenue approach' to key buildings
2. Fortification: a means of defending the settlement during the many wars of the period
3. Garden design: linking formal parks and public gardens by tree-lined avenues into and through the city
4. The place: the creation of settings and enclosures for statues, buildings and other objects
5. The squared grid layout: chessboard arrangement derived from Greek and colonial Roman settlements merging into radial and concentric patterns

In England around the 16th century, a substantial increase in population,[3] combined with massive inflation in the price of food[4] and the new availability of land for investment,[5] resulted in huge changes to the landscape, to settlements and for people. Narrow, winding medieval streets were not suited to the increased use by horse-drawn carriages, which caused damage to surface paving and conflicted with pedestrians. This resulted in the creation of wider streets with segregated footpaths, more formalised street layout and intersections and road straightening to allow quicker movement from A to B. Changes were facilitated by a growing awareness of the 'street' as being something more than just a thoroughfare through a town: 'it was the town itself' (Sharp, 1938: 33), and was created by architects working together with enlightened landowners rather than a central governing town planning authority; Inigo Jones (1573–1652) being the principal proponent of Renaissance architecture and town planning in Britain (Burke, 1975: 99).

Town planning in Britain during this time was generally concerned with 'piecemeal additions on fields or gardens or replacement of medieval slums' (Burke, 1975: 108); it was rarely involved in the development of new towns or large-scale urban expansions. Unlike in continental Europe, where strong monarchy was shaping town design, the dispersed nature of the British aristocracy and the power of merchants dominated the layout of settlements. This resulted in 'a distinctive form of town planning: the development of formal residential quarters consisting of dignified houses built in terraces or rows, generally on a strong geometric street plan', interspersed by formal parks, squares and gardens (Hall and Tewdwr-Jones, 2010: 12). Examples include Bath (incorporating the creation of the Royal Crescent) and Edinburgh (the building of the New Town area), both of which were experiencing population growth pressures, though neither of these schemes could be said to be providing wider direct community benefit. The increasing segregation between rich and poor was exacerbated by the grand style of redevelopment. However, despite these shortcomings, this period has been heralded as a 'golden age for British town planning' (Burke, 1975: 114).

This is not to say that regulation associated with monarchy was not occurring in the UK. Indeed, the monarchy, in parallel with increasing parliamentary power, led to a number of key developments in the development of regulation concerning the built environment. Examples of this can be found in association with Elizabeth I, James I and Charles I who, between them, are associated with a variety of Proclamations and Acts that considered health, safety, density, resources and aesthetics. These were still limited in scope, geography and impact, but again we see the slow development of regulatory controls taking place (Sheppard et al, 2017).

In the countryside, the quality of English manufactured woollen cloth was a significant factor in generating wealth, resulting in an ever-increasing demand for sheep pasture. The sale of monastic lands[6] provided a timely opportunity for already large landowners to further expand their estates for keeping sheep. The enclosure of land by fences and hedgerows to corral livestock and to grow specific crops created a patchwork of fields, which became a feature of the English landscape still in existence today. But this was at a significant social cost: the large-scale farming units required to deliver efficiencies meant that smaller farmers and their workers were evicted from their lands. In contrast, large country houses set within parks and gardens (at first formal and then as stylised landscapes) began appearing across the landscape during the 17th and 18th centuries, signalling the rise of the 'landscape architect'.[7]

The Industrial Revolution, health considerations and 'model' settlements

The mechanisation of labour in the countryside resulted in migration of disposed rural workers to urban factories and mills. The population of towns increased significantly,[8] especially those in the north and midlands of England. Housing all of these people was a significant problem, though not one that employers or local councils considered within their remit (Burke, 1975: 127). Housing was therefore constructed by speculative builders. Back-to-back houses were cheap to erect and made efficient use of the land available, since they only had a single façade facing the light and air, the other three forming the side walls of adjacent dwellings (see Figure 2.4).

Figure 2.4: Cross-section of a typical back-to-back house

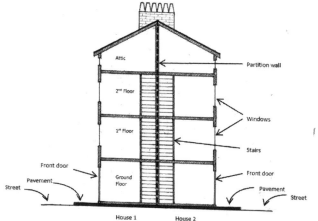

These houses consequentially lacked light and ventilation, a contributory factor of tuberculosis. They were also devoid of water supply and basic sewerage, and were often overcrowded, with multiple generations of a family living in the same room. The communal toilets and water standpipes were breeding grounds for waterborne diseases such as typhus and cholera. Public health was a major issue at this time.

Improvements in the transportation of goods across Britain, firstly by the creation of canal waterways in the 18th century and then by railways in the 19th century, unfortunately worsened the health impacts in urban areas. The arrival of coal-driven steam railways into towns exacerbated public health crises – Abercrombie (1933) noted that railways were 'hailed as the prime symbol of industrial success' and thus were afforded 'despotic powers', resulting in other aspects of the built environment being overlooked. Those who could afford to vacate the squalor of towns for the suburbs and rural villages did so, leaving their formerly resplendent Georgian terraces deteriorating through multiple occupation by poorer families, thereby amplifying the disjuncture between rich and poor (Burke, 1975: 130).

At the time there was also a movement of philanthropists who sought to improve their workers' physical and social conditions through the construction of model villages. Robert Owen (1771–1858) acquired New Lanark, Scotland, in 1799 to house the workers for his cotton mill. He also sought to improve their morality by providing a school, cooperative shop and levying fines for drunkenness, among other rules. There are other examples too: Titus Salt built Saltaire, near Bradford (1851); W. H. Lever Brothers built Port Sunlight, near Liverpool (1888); and the Cadbury family built Bourneville, near Birmingham (1893). The latter two are notable in town planning terms for the extensive public open space that was incorporated within them. The economic incentive for the builders' actions was that a contented workforce would be more productive and thus increase financial profits.

Going beyond the village scale, James Silk Buckingham's (1786–1855) designs for a new town called Victoria, set out in his book *National Evils and Practical Remedies* (1849), was intended to house up to ten thousand people (Karakiewicz et al, 2015: 64). His intentions, although never realised, were to construct a small town that contained 'every improvement in its position, plan, drainage, ventilation, architecture, supply of water, light and every other elegance and convenience' (Buckingham, 1849: 142–3).

These small-scale examples, though important in demonstrating how planning for communities could be carried out, were the exception rather than the rule. Victorian towns and cities were still crowded, dirty and unhealthy places in which to live. The first Public Health Act 1848 came about following a report by Edwin Chadwick on *The Sanitary Conditions of the Labouring Population of Great Britain* (1842). It sought to improve the sanitary conditions of towns through combating waterborne diseases arising from the juxtaposition of water supply, sewerage and drainage, by placing environmental health regulation under a single local body; however, a severe limitation was that it did not actually require any action.[9] Outbreaks of cholera in Britain remained frequent and serious. John Snow's mapping of occurrences of cholera around Soho, London, in 1854 identified a link between the disease and the proximity of water standpipes (from which the inhabitants drew their drinking water) and pollution from sewage. This realisation led, in part, to a further Public Health Act in 1875, which required running water and drainage to be incorporated into all new houses. It also required a higher standard of overall construction and street layout, which would be controlled through locally created by-laws that set standard room sizes and road widths (Abercrombie, 1933: 78). These terraced dwellings were designed as 'through houses' with front and rear windows and tunnels between every four houses to give access to rear yards where private toilets ('privies') were located.

The emergence of these strict by-laws is an important step in the development of a planning system in the UK. Here we see a regulatory system emerge which required conformity with standards, a prescribed approach to planning, and one very different in approach to the one we find in place today.

The quality of by-law terraces improved over time but the regimented ramrod-straight street layout, and lack of greenery or respect for topographic features, resulted in very limited visual interest. Sitte (1889) was strongly critical of the geometric 'planned' redevelopment of urban areas wholly on the basis of drainage, sewerage and traffic flow, and instead 'sought to recapture the accidental beauty of the medieval urban scene' (Burke: 1975: 152). Similarly, Abercrombie noted that by-law housing had 'planned away every feature of natural interest and beauty' (1933: 78).

> The triumph of sanitary reform was soured by the dreary monotony of bricks and mortar and asphalt, grim lack of amenity, playgrounds or open space, and the virtual destruction of every tree, hedge and blade of grass. (Burke, 1975: 144)

The garden city movement

The antidote to the lack of greenery in urban areas was the 'garden city', proposed by Ebenezer Howard in his book *To-morrow: A Peaceful Path to Real Reform* (1898) (later republished in 1902 under its better-known title *Garden Cities of Tomorrow*). His ideas were influenced by the model villages and sought to incorporate the best of both town and country, encapsulated through his 'Three Magnets diagram' showing how the polar opposites could be successfully combined (see Figure 2.5). In contrast to the by-law housing, garden cities were to provide a variety of housing types with their own private gardens and broad road widths planted with trees and grass verges, resulting in a much lower density: 'the sign of the penetration of the country into the town' (Abercrombie, 1933: 86).

The garden city was based on the premise of collective cooperative benefit: purchasing land at agricultural values, with the financial proceeds of development being ploughed back into improving community facilities. There would be a network of garden cities, surrounded by wide belts of agricultural land to prevent urban sprawl, each having a population of around thirty thousand, which was linked by rail and road to a larger central city of around fifty-eight thousand people (see Figure 2.6). In applying garden *city* ideas to existing towns and cities the notion of the garden *suburb* was born.

Figure 2.5: Ebenezer Howard's Three Magnets diagram used to illustrate the attraction of urban and rural attributes

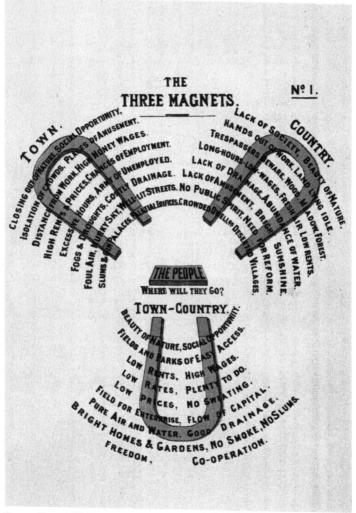

Source: Howard (1898).

These were to be extensions to urban areas incorporating many of the residential ideals but connected to a parent city. New Earswick, York (1902) was the first but the most famous is Hampstead Garden Suburb, London (1904).

The first garden city was constructed at Letchworth (1903) by architects Raymond Unwin and Barry Parker. Their plan was zonal: industrial and residential areas were kept separate; public buildings and shopping were provided in the centre, with housing radiating out in concentric circles (see Figure 2.7).

Figure 2.6: Garden cities surrounding a central city – note how they are indicatively separated by agricultural fields and other 'open' land

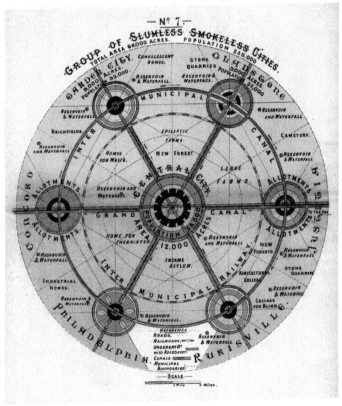

Source: Howard (1898).

Figure 2.7 The garden city with radial zones

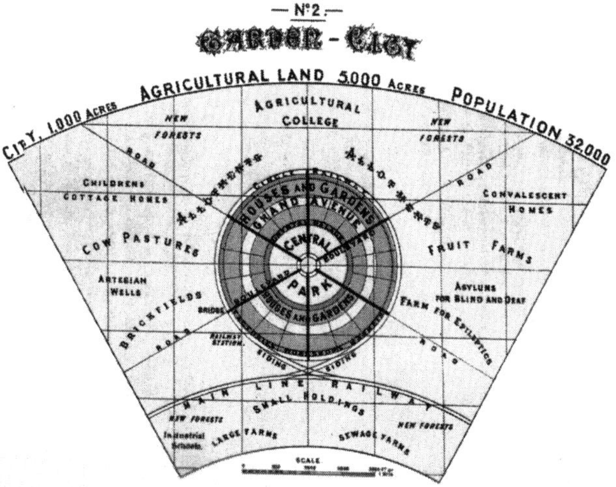

Source: Howard (1898).

In 1920 a second garden city, Welwyn Garden City, was begun which took on board earlier good practice from Letchworth and was more true to Howard's initial concept. The subsequent popularity of garden cities and model villages, as well as examples from other countries (the US and Germany), demonstrated in practical terms how a well-planned environment could bring about economic, social and environmental improvements for all concerned. Critics have since argued that the low density coupled with the desire for individual gardens has in part been responsible for urban sprawl.

It was around this time that the term 'town planning' was first used,[10] providing a useful, politically neutral, term to describe an activity that, while previously considered the pursuit of left-wing reformists, was being accepted as a societally beneficial and necessary element of arranging the places in which people lived and worked (Ward, 2004: 25). Consequentially, the garden city movement was influential in bringing about legislative formality for town and country planning (Burke, 1975: 147), and Howard's book remains 'one of the most important books in the history of urban planning' (Hall and Tewdwr-Jones, 2010: 28).

Planning in the 20th century

Our story in the second half of the chapter presents a journey through the decades, punctuated, regularly, by legislative planning Acts.

The first reference to town planning in statute came about in the Housing, Town Planning etc. Act 1909, which empowered local authorities to produce Town Planning Schemes (plans) to secure sanitary improvements in the laying out of land. Patrick Geddes (1854–1932) was influential in introducing the 'survey – analysis – plan' notion of needing to survey a location before preparing a plan for its future development. The emphasis of action was now less on grand artistic development schemes and more on 'density, zoning, site layouts and civic design' (Ward, 2004: 33). In terms of housing densities, Unwin's book *Nothing Gained by Overcrowding* (1912) advised on residential standards. However, Town Planning Schemes were convoluted to prepare and only applied to new developments, not those which already existed, so they did not address existing problems. They were 'regulatory devices' to address basic living standards rather than provide positive forward planning. Crucially, they were voluntary to prepare – by 1914 only 56 schemes had been produced (Poxon, 2000: 75) – and difficult for planning authorities to enforce owing to the liability to pay developers compensation.

The significance of the Act was that it introduced town planning as a profession rather than something to be done on a voluntary basis by social reformers (Ward, 2004: 32). Engineers and surveyors took on the function of town planning in local government, while architects and lawyers from the private sector also had an interest (Ward, 2004: 32). Formal planning education was begun at the University of Liverpool in 1909 and the Town Planning Institute (later to be renamed the Royal Town Planning Institute, RTPI) was created in 1913–14.

The 1920s

Although the First World War (1914–18) caused a temporary pause in large-scale construction, building work continued rapidly afterwards with some 1.1 million council houses built in the interwar period and 2.7 million private sector homes delivered in the 1930s (TCPA, 2017: 2). The Tudor Walters Committee Report (1918) sought to improve living standards by setting housing densities at 12 houses per acre (30 per hectare), reflecting the model of garden suburb extensions to existing urban areas rather than creating new standalone settlements. This approach was formalised in the Housing, Town Planning, etc. Act 1919 by providing homes "fit for heroes to live in".[11] It also incorporated experiments in state intervention for working-class housing (council estates) but building at lower density necessitated using greenfield sites on the periphery of towns, thus contributing to the spread of urbanisation. The Campaign to Protect Rural England (CPRE), formed in 1926 out of concern about urban sprawl, became a significant pressure group lobbying against development in the countryside.

Despite all of these Acts coming into force, the basis for town planning was still narrowly conceived, with 'local authorities struggling to balance flexibility with rigidity' (Poxon, 2000: 75). This has been a reoccurring theme throughout the decades and is still a tension in the current operation of the UK's various planning systems.

The 1930s

The Town and Country Planning Act 1932 extended planning powers to cover almost any land (built-up or greenfield), which effectively created a zoning approach for managing new development (see Chapter 6 on managing development). However, the planning system at the time was fragmented and lacked the tools to require that necessary social infrastructure be incorporated into developments. Developers were increasingly siting their new housing along the main highways leading out of towns, as it reduced the need for expenditure on new roads. This 'ribbon development' was very damaging to the visual appearance of the countryside, and as housing was spread out without land being allocated for public/community facilities, it meant these had to be provided in locations remote from those who would be using them. The Restriction of Ribbon Development Act 1935 sought to prevent such linear development.

In the 1930s the north–south economic divide was established, and deepening. Migrating labour from the declining industrial North of England led to a housing boom in the South East and Midlands. In response, 'planned decentralization and containment' along the lines conceptualised by Howard was adopted for managing urban growth in the interwar period (Ward, 2004: 36). The containment of large urban areas, such that their growth could be directed towards satellite towns, was dependent on the definition of their boundaries. The urban fringe was particularly susceptible to differing interpretations, so protection via the concept of the highly restrictive 'green belt' was conceived, initially for the areas around London, through the Green Belt Act 1938 (see section below).

Planning in the interwar years was essentially only being done at a local level, but there was a shift in attitudes in the late 1930s from a laissez-faire approach to one of greater state intervention (Ward, 2004: 70). The main drivers for this encompassed social, economic and environmental concerns, such as increasing suburbanisation, traffic congestion, unemployment and poverty (Ward, 2004: 71). A desire to address regional imbalances through more comprehensive planning, as exemplified by the government's Commission on the Distribution of the Industrial Population (1937), culminating in the Barlow Report (1940), represented a shift from planning at a localised level to one of national concern by advocating the decentralisation of population. Despite initially being put aside due to the Second World War, the report can be considered 'the single most important policy document in British planning history' (Ward, 2004: 80).

Around the same time, a number of other reports were commissioned by the government in recognition that having a system of comprehensive physical land use planning was something that was in the nation's best interests to overcome the market failures that were 'having a chronic impact on people's welfare' (TCPA, 2017: 3). Examples include the Scott Committee 1942 report on rural land use, the Uthwatt Committee 1942 report on compensation between land market and the state, and the Reith Commission 1945 report on setting up development corporations for New Towns. In summary, 'during the period from the 19th century through to the 1947 Act the planning system evolved from an ad hoc concern with issues of public health and social unrest to a comprehensive attempt to instil order into the management of land use' (Rydin: 1993: 31).

Conclusions

In this chapter we have charted the development of the act and art of planning from its early origins in a diversity of legislation and practice through to an actual system which identifies itself as 'planning'. The drivers of this evolution are numerous, but a combination of both public and private interests can be seen as key influences in each step taken. This chapter ended with the foundations for a new system to provide a comprehensive and universal planning system, which would shortly be established and which will be explored in the next chapter.

Further reading

For comprehensive consideration and examples of the development of medieval English towns, the following texts are recommended:

Burke, G. (1975) *Towns in the making*, London: Edward Arnold.
Platt, C. (1976) *The English medieval town*, London: Secker and Warburg.

A detailed consideration of the interwar years and the rise of the modern planning approach can be found in:

Ward, S. (2004) *Planning and urban change* (2nd edn), London: SAGE Publications Ltd.

Notes

1 Roman Empire: 753 BC – AD 476.

2 For the purposes of this section we are referring to 'medieval' and 'Middle Ages' interchangeably, to cover the period from the Norman Conquest until the 14th century.

3 The population in England doubled between the mid-15th and mid-17th centuries (Platt, 1976: 175).

4 Prices for food had increased six-fold between 1500 and 1630 (Platt, 1976: 175).

5 As a consequence of Henry VIII's dissolution of the monasteries in 1535–36.

6 As a consequence of Henry VIII's dissolution of the monasteries in 1535–36.

7 Humphry Repton (1752–1818) was the first to use the term 'landscape architect', but Lancelot 'Capability' Brown (1715–83) was the most famous.

8 Between 1801 and 1901 the population of England and Wales increased from 8.9 to 32.5 million (Burke, 1975: 126).

9 UK Parliament online, available at www.parliament.uk

10 The term 'town planning' apparently first arose in 1905 in a discussion between the chairman of Birmingham's Housing Committee (John Nettlefold) and its Medical Officer of Health (John Robertson) (described in Ward, 2004: 25, citing Adams, 1929, and King, 1982).

11 Election pledge in 1918 by David Lloyd George (who subsequently became Prime Minister).

3

Post-war history

Introduction

The preceding chapter took us on a journey to the establishment of a comprehensive planning system in the UK. It is at the emergence of this, which occurred during and immediately following one of the most significant periods of UK history, that we now pick up the story. In this chapter we will see how the system was born, and then, having been established, how it evolved into the modern and current systems of planning we find in place today.

Planning after the Second World War: the Town and Country Planning Act 1947

The Second World War resulted in significant damage to many towns and cities in the UK. The rebuilding of these cities, alongside containment of urban sprawl, required more effective planning controls than had previously been in place. The Town and Country Planning Act 1947 provided the tools for local planning authorities to undertake the necessary reshaping of many towns, including the incorporation of new road systems within urban areas to take account of the increasing prevalence of the motor vehicle, without fear of landowner claims for significant compensation.

The 1947 Act heralded the birth of modern planning and is seen as a 'major landmark in planning history ... for the first time it allowed local planning authorities to produce outcomes significantly different from what would have happened without planning' (Ward, 2004: 101) (see Box 3.1).

Box 3.1: Key elements of the Town and Country Planning Act 1947

- Nationalised development rights
- Development required planning permission, which could be refused or conditioned
- Simplification of compulsory purchase of land procedures
- County planning authorities to prepare a development plan based on a survey and analysis of their area
- Permitted development rights for agriculture and forestry
- Control over new large-scale industrial development
- Strengthening powers to protect heritage by 'listing' buildings of architectural or historic interest
- Preservation of amenity and woodland

The Act fundamentally shaped the approach to organising our built and natural environment by nationalising development rights, which effectively required anyone that wished to undertake development (including changing the use of land) to apply for permission to do so. The local planning authority (a role given to the county councils rather than the districts, which significantly reduced the number of planning authorities) had discretion to refuse, approve or impose conditions on development without the worry of having to compensate the developer (see Chapter 6 on development management). This meant that planning could be undertaken in the 'public interest' rather than being driven by the private sector market. Decisions were to be based upon, but not tied to, the content of the development plan that local planning authorities were required to prepare for their administrative area. The system, therefore, was now not based upon regulatory plans, which required conformity, but on policy, which required consideration and a decision that was to be taken on its merits (Sheppard et al, 2017). This change of approach from the regulatory zonal system of planning schemes to the discretionary system of development plans has remained in place ever since (see Chapters 5 and 6).

The involvement of the public in planning decisions at this time was viewed as an afterthought, something to be sought once the planners had arrived at the 'correct' outcome in the public interest. This is one of the 1947 Act's main weaknesses, as it alienated the public on whose behalf the actions were being undertaken. Coupled with this, the system was not delivering on its promise to remediate the housing shortage, such that 'planning [was] now appearing to be part of the problem rather than the solution' (Ward, 2004: 104).

Subsequent Planning Acts in 1953, 1954, 1959 and 1963, as well as a host of other related legislation in between, effectively tweaked and weakened the planning system each time. The financial provisions were restructured to make development a more attractive proposition for the market, thus rebalancing the relationship between public interest and private wealth accumulation. Planning's reduced role in the 1950s, despite the introduction of new towns (see below), reflected a move politically in favour of the private sector and the development of a mixed economy. A loosely formed consensus between those involved from all sides ensured planning's survival, albeit weakened.

The rise of the new towns in the 1950s

Following the Second World War there was a need for physical and social reconstruction. Coupled with a desire to decentralise industry and an aim to rehouse the population from overcrowded slums in the main urban areas, this provided the driving force behind the creation of planned new towns across the UK. The New Towns Act 1946 paved the way for locations to be designated in three 'waves': 1946–55, 1961–64 and 1967–71 (see Table 3.1).

New towns had their origins in the garden city movement, albeit without the cooperative land ownership aspect or the link to a larger central city. Each town was to be built by a development corporation and to be largely self-sufficient in terms of jobs for its population of up to 50,000 people. Neighbourhood units were planned around the

Table 3.1: New towns in the UK

Mark 1: first wave (1946–55)	Mark 2: second wave (1961–64)	Mark 3: third wave (1967–71)
Stevenage	Redditch	Milton Keynes
Crawley	Livingston	Peterborough*
Hemel Hempstead	Skelmersdale	Northampton*
Harlow	Runcorn	Ipswich* (later dropped)
Welwyn and Hatfield	Warrington*	Telford (formerly Dawley)
Basildon	Leyland and Chorley	Central Lancashire* (Preston)
Bracknell	Washington	
Newton Aycliffe	Killingworth	
Peterlee	Cramlington	
East Kilbride	Irvine	
Glenrothes		
Cwmbran		
Corby		
Cumbernauld		

*Towns expanded under the New Towns Act 1946.

provision of schools, shops, healthcare and open space. They were to contain a mix of housing types to provide a balanced community of social classes. Industrial employment areas were zoned away from the residential neighbourhoods, which radiated out from the town centre containing the civic, commercial and cultural buildings.

The design of new towns recognised the need to plan for an increase in motorised traffic. Extensive use was made of 'Radburn'-style housing layouts in which pedestrians and vehicles were physically segregated, especially within the town centre: Stevenage (1956) was the first fully purpose-built pedestrianised town centre in the UK (Burke, 1975: 165), while the Lijnbaan, Rotterdam (1953) was the first in Europe (see Figure 3.1).

With regards to housing, the Radburn approach is typified by houses fronting onto grassed areas where entry was solely pedestrian. Vehicular access and garaging was provided to the rear of properties. This approach was later discredited due to the prevalence for

Figure 3.1: The Lijnbaan, Rotterdam, Europe's first purpose-built pedestrianised shopping street with residential development behind the shops

Photograph: Croft, N.

antisocial behaviour to occur in the rear access roads where there was limited surveillance (see Figures 3.2, 3.3 and 3.4).

Delivering a new town is a significant undertaking and, at least initially, progress was slow (Wannop, 1999: 214). Despite early setbacks, the programme continued throughout the next two decades, finally ending around the mid-1970s. This approach to building new communities contributed 'the greatest level of housebuilding in the history of the nation' (TCPA, 2017: 5). Between 1945 and 1991, 1 in 25 of all dwellings constructed in the UK was in a new town and some 1.4 million inhabitants had been accommodated (Wannop, 1999: 213). Despite these successes, however, there was an overall lack of strategic planning in the post-war period. At a national level, the various government ministries that impacted directly upon land use were uncoordinated; at a more local scale, there was very limited cooperation between local authorities. This resulted in a somewhat patchy quality to the delivery of planning functions, which in turn fuelled concerns that planning was not effectively connecting with people.

Figure 3.2: An indicative plan showing a Radburn-style housing development

Figure 3.3: An example of a Radburn-style housing development

Photograph: Croft, N.

Figure 3.4: Rear access road and garages in a Radburn-style housing development

Photograph: Croft, N.

Urban containment policies

Green belt is the most widely recognised containment policy in the UK. Closely aligned with the garden city approach, although now fulfilling different functions, green belt policy seeks to contain urban areas from sprawling out into surrounding rural land. Other purposes now include preserving the character of towns, preventing nearby settlements from merging and ensuring that accessible green space is retained for recreation. In seeking to achieve these goals, it has the fundamental aim of preventing unacceptable development, which is pretty much any kind of built form (with a few exceptions).

The first green belt was designated around London in 1938 and formed part of Patrick Abercrombie's London Plan (1943). The 1947 Act subsequently allowed other local planning authorities to include designated green belt proposals in their plans, and in 1955 the Housing Minster Duncan Sandys actively encouraged such designations through Circular 42/55. Designated green belt land, a key feature of which is its permanence, now accounts for some ten per cent of land in the UK (Cullingworth et al, 2015: 403). The near blanket ban it imposes on new development makes it a readily understandable concept for the lay person and it is the most enduring, and publicly supported, of all planning policies, albeit misunderstood by many. It is perhaps due to this simplicity and level of public support that successive governments of varying political persuasions have to a large extent resisted incursions within it, particularly in the run-up to general elections.

The policy approach for managing proposals for development on green belt land was set out in the government's Planning Policy Guidance Note 2 (1988), and subsequently in the National Planning Policy Framework (2012), both of which largely followed the original policy approach from the 1950s. However, over many decades there has been pressure for green belt boundaries to be reviewed and new approaches (such as green wedges) to be tried, to allow urban expansion to accommodate a growing population. If further densification of towns and cities is unpalatable, one alternative to expanding existing areas is to create new ones.

Planning in the 1960s

Planning in the 1960s was dominated by the rise in use of the motor vehicle and an increasing desire for greater public participation in planning decision-making. The report *Traffic in Towns* (the 'Buchanan Report', 1963) was considered a 'great milestone in town planning techniques' (Burke, 1975: 174) in that it recognised and sought to address issues around increased accessibility while reducing congestion and retaining a high-quality environment for pedestrians. It acknowledged that while there was an inevitability about the growth in car usage, urban areas could not absorb that rise indefinitely. Importantly, as a planning approach, the report explicitly linked transport planning with land use and development at a time when the government administered those functions through separate departments (Ward, 2004: 136).

In the 1960s there were also renewed concerns about housing shortages due to the inadequacy of large proportions of the existing stock combined with anticipated population increases (Ward, 2004:

111). Public involvement in planning was becoming increasingly driven by two competing but linked factors: the displacement of communities via slum clearance schemes and a desire to prevent encroachment into surrounding countryside (as previously noted through green belt policy). In terms of the former, the replacement of terraced back-to-back housing with tower-block flats as a solution to overcrowded inner-city areas and a shortage in housing supply began in the 1950s and gained pace during the 1960s, but by the late 1960s/70s it was being discredited due to poor-quality structural build, lack of maintenance, social segregation and the splitting up of communities, and lack of recreation space for families.

The first major overhaul of the 1947 planning system came about following the recommendations of the Planning Advisory Group (PAG), comprising public and private representatives at local and national level, which was established by the government to recommend how development plans, while comprehensive in coverage, could be made more flexible in dealing with change. The group's subsequent report (PAG, 1965) made a distinction between overarching issues, which could be identified through a 'two-tiered' arrangement, in strategic 'structure plans', and more specific tactical interventions undertaken on a site-by-site basis in 'Local Plans' (Ward, 2004: 122; Cullingworth et al, 2015: 108). This formed the basis for the Town and Country Planning Act 1968, which initially envisaged the two tiers of plans being created by a single planning authority in each area. However, the 1972 restructuring of local authorities ended in a division of functions, including planning, between the larger counties and their smaller constituent districts/ boroughs. This fragmentation of planning responsibilities still remains today.

Another important aspect of the 1968 Act, at least in terms of the principles it embodied, was the inclusion of measures to improve public involvement in the preparation of development plans following the Skeffington Report (1969) (see Chapter 4). This reflected wider civil desire for greater power in decision-making. However, the outcome was less progressive than might have been expected, with the participatory procedures being largely related to keeping people informed and requesting comments on draft documents (Cullingworth et al, 2015: 509).

Planning approaches in the 1970s

The global economy was changing in the 1970s and, as wider competition entered the market, the traditional British manufacturing industry did not adapt well, resulting in its decline. Particularly hard hit were those areas that heavily relied on manufacturing to support local jobs, and rising unemployment was a major issue. The previously supported cross-party consensus for a mixed economy began to disintegrate (Ward, 2004: 176). In the mid-1970s Britain joined the European Union (at the time it was the European Economic Community, 1973) though there was scepticism about having closer ties with European countries from those who saw Britain as capable and strong enough to act as an independent state.

The Town and Country Planning Act 1971 allowed local planning authorities to seek 'planning gain' to fund infrastructure related to new development (at the time called 'section 52 agreements', but later to become better known as section 106 agreements under the 1990 Act). The basic premise that planning permission cannot be bought or sold was a key concern in this aspect, but one that has become an important and necessary part of the development process. Planning approaches in the 1970s moved away from an all-encompassing redevelopment of inner-urban areas to more targeted interventionist methods with social aspects at the forefront, characterised through local authorities identifying Housing Action Areas to improve living conditions (Cullingworth et al, 2015: 427). However, the post-war legacy of comprehensive inner-city redevelopment had given planning and planners a bad name, such that by the late 1970s the incoming Thatcherite government's ideological opposition to state control sought a significant change in policy direction.

The 1980s: free-market planning

The 1980s approach to planning was characterised by a government that favoured the free-market economy and the pursuit of individual wealth. Such an attitude did not sit easily with a planning system that sought to operate in the 'public interest'. 'Market principles were advocated as a way both to create new wealth and to give people what they actually wanted, rather than what planners or other professional bureaucrats thought they needed' (Ward, 2004: 186). State intervention in the operation of the market and social welfare was rolled back. Additionally, residents of council housing were offered the 'right to buy' their properties, which reduced the availability of affordable housing.

The government's opinion of planning at the time was revealed by the title of their White Paper *Lifting the Burden* (1985). Measures to streamline planning requirements included creation of Simplified Planning Zones (SPZs) and revisions to the Use Classes Order (see Chapter 6 on development management), although in the case of the former the take-up was somewhat underwhelming.[1] Upper-tier metropolitan councils were removed to reduce the size and power of local government,[2] and people's involvement in planning was 'no longer characterised as due process but as "delay" and the cost-benefit equation for development was burdened with the transactional costs of planning without weighing the wider public benefits into the equation' (TCPA, 2017: 8).

The planning system (including those working within it) was seen by the Thatcherite government as being a bureaucratic obstruction to the free market and wealth generation. There were, however, those who simultaneously applauded the levels of constraint offered in terms of protecting rural areas from urban sprawl and safeguarding aspects such as ecology and heritage. Many 'ordinary' people also sought environmental protection for the value it afforded in safeguarding their immediate environs: pejoratively labelled as the 'Not In My Back Yard' (NIMBY) brigade. The potential contradiction between allowing the market a free run and environmental preservation for core home-owning voters caused a dichotomy for the ruling Conservative government, which has persisted ever since.

The 'solution' was seen in part as reducing the strategic comprehensiveness of planning and replacing it with a more piecemeal set of specific interventions under the Local Government, Planning and Land Act 1980: Urban Development Corporations took over planning responsibilities in particular locations, and specific designated Enterprise Zones removed nearly all planning constraints altogether. However, concerns that decisions on more local-scale planning applications were becoming increasingly unpredictable led to a growing realisation that uncertainty was more of a burden to the development industry than a predictable regulatory planning system.

The 1990s: sustainability and the plan-led system

The government's response to what it saw as maverick unpredictable decisions on development proposals being taken by 'amateurs in town halls' was to reaffirm the plan-led approach to decision-making. The Town and Country Planning Act 1990 (alongside the Planning and Compensation Act 1991) placed development plans on a statutory footing. This gave the plan primacy in determining planning applications, albeit with the discretionary element of 'material considerations' (see Chapter 6 on development plans and policy). 'In theory, [development plans] play a strategic, integrating and coordinating role and provide a degree of certainty and consistency in decision-making' (Cullingworth et al, 2015: 107). The confirmation of the government's commitment to a plan-led system signalled an end to the Thatcherite crusade against planning.

The 1990s also saw a rise in the terminology of 'sustainability' and 'sustainable development', two nebulous and notoriously difficult-to-define terms. They were popular with those wanting to extol the virtues of their proposal, or those wanting to object to it, as arguments could be prefixed with the term sustainable/unsustainable without seemingly having to justify it further. It simultaneously meant all things to all people. Notwithstanding this, or possibly because of its political expedience, the notion of sustainability has become a key concept, based upon the three equal 'pillars' of social, economic and environmental concerns.

Despite an ideology seeking less state intervention, the government prepared more and more Planning Policy Guidance Notes (PPGs) covering a wide range of subjects (for example, subjects as diverse as transport, noise, archaeology, tourism, telecommunications) to guide local planning authorities on what to put in their plans. The elevated importance of the development plan, however, came at a price. The preparation process increased in significance, and with it came a rise in the amount of supporting material and activities required to justify a particular position. Those parties with a particular interest in a parcel of land would invest longer in preparing and sifting through the evidence underpinning a plan. Planning inquiries into development plans consequently increased in length – famously, Leeds Unitary Development Plan took nearly ten years to be adopted (Cullingworth et al, 2015: 113) – resulting in plans that were potentially outdated before they were adopted (Ward, 2004: 240). The planning application process was similarly criticised for causing delay and uncertainty.

The 2000s: the 'spatial planning' project

Just as each previous decade had been marked by a planning Act, the 2000s was no different. As we've seen, planning was already at the behest of political whims, but it gained renewed political attention during the New Labour years (1997–2010) through instigation of the 'spatial planning' approach. This was intended to be a 'new' way of reinvigorating development by facilitating rather than regulating development. The planning profession thus found itself placed centre stage in the drive to solve the country's social, economic and environmental woes.

The Planning and Compulsory Purchase Act 2004 sought to address perceived delay and uncertainty in planning processes primarily by reforming the development plan preparation process. This involved creating a portfolio of shorter documents,[3] collectively referred to as a Local Development Framework (LDF), which could be prepared and individually updated in a more timely fashion. Regional Spatial Strategies were to provide the strategic context prepared by a regional tier of governance (Regional Assemblies – see Chapter 4).

In tandem, the planning application process was recast as 'managing' rather than 'controlling' development. This 'new' direction was viewed by many involved in handling planning applications as effectively normalising what was currently already operating as best practice. A more concerning turn was the encouragement for planners to be the facilitators of development – to unblock obstructions in the system. On the face of it this sat in stark contrast to planners' role as arbiters between competing interests. However, in reality the system did not operate in such a black-and-white manner. Instead, planners were advised to consider themselves proactively operating at the *hub of a wheel*, with the planner coordinating efforts between many other professions and joining up policy initiatives to deliver sustainable development: a laudable, if optimistic, view of how the system should operate given its domination by private sector development finance.

Again, however, the practical reality did not meet the intended outcome, with delays in the preparation of plans remaining prevalent across the country (for example, preparation of the *Gloucester, Cheltenham and Tewkesbury Joint Core Strategy* commenced in July 2008 and it was finally adopted in December 2017), the process across the country being heavily dominated by the need to collect evidence on which to appraise options. The seemingly insatiable desire for planning inquiries to explore every avenue of investigation caused the system to procrastinate, although it was one that pressure groups opposed to development would consider a price worth paying to avoid the damaging consequences of development. Government advice that the evidence required only needed to be 'proportionate' did little to assuage those seeking to discredit another party's position. Proportionate in the case of planning inquiries/appeals was relative to the amount of material provided by the opposing party, resulting in the production of an accretion of supporting information.

The belief that 'spatial planning could deliver consensus-based, high-quality, place-sensitive sustainable development ... was something that few initially questioned' (Haughton and Allmendinger, 2011: 184). Anyone doubting this mantra was labelled 'old-school' and out of touch. The collective planning profession's hubris[4] sought outcomes that the regulatory planning process struggled to provide, as ultimately the system remained heavily reliant on the private sector to deliver its objectives (as it had been since its inception). A main concern for some, and one that had been building since the 1950s, was the perceived lack of 'real' community involvement in decision-making. The next incarnation of the planning system was intended to dramatically change that.

Localism post 2010

The spatial planning approach was perceived by government as not having delivered on expectations. Consequently, the terminology was seen as politically tainted and was quietly swept under the carpet (Allmendinger and Houghton, 2011: 186). The Localism Act 2011 (England) put community planning on a formal statutory footing, with greater emphasis placed on the tiers of governance at the level closest to the place of development impact, providing the opportunity for parishes and community forums to prepare neighbourhood plans and create Neighbourhood Development Orders and community right to build schemes. The community planners involved often comprise a range of professionals who reside in the neighbourhood supported by an eclectic mix of 'Dad's Army' armchair enthusiasts keen to retain the character of their village/town and urban activists determined to pursue a particular agenda such as precluding commercialisation and/or gentrification.

The perceived democratic deficit of Regional Spatial Strategies resulted in them being scrapped in 2010 in favour of a 'duty to cooperate' between adjacent districts to deliver housing and economic development. A return to Local Plans as a single point of reference for developers and communities, as opposed to LDF portfolios, coupled with the replacement of 50,000 pages of government planning statements into the "great précis"[5] that is the National Planning Policy Framework (NPPF, 2012), has generally been seen as a positive move in simplifying England's planning system. However, the NPPF's presumption in favour of sustainable development, and the consideration of financial 'viability' in deciding the extent to which policies need to be adhered to, has redistributed the equality between the three 'pillars' of sustainability by placing greater emphasis on the economic element in an attempt to increase the supply of housing. Additionally, there has been an increase in the breadth and range of matters benefiting from permitted development rights to convert agricultural buildings and offices into residential accommodation regardless of their suitability and location. All of these measures have been introduced in an attempt to free up the planning system, largely in order to deliver the housing that the country needs. The first revision of the NPPF occurred in July 2018, and while it largely rolls forward the previous approach, it adds commentary on a standardised national housing needs methodology and housing delivery testing for individual councils. Once again, the necessity to increase the levels of housebuilding in England is at its forefront.

Conclusions: tensions in the system

This short guide to the history of planning will inevitably be unable to cover every single aspect of this diverse subject. However, in the preceding discussion we have set out those aspects that we consider to be salient in telling the story of planning in the UK.

Planning in the UK as we know it really begins after the Second World War. One of the most striking things about the UK's modern planning regime is that it has been under 'near constant change' since its inception in 1947 (TCPA, 2017: 5). Only at certain times were previous approaches and policy consolidated, so the accumulation of changes to both process and content without wiping away what went before has led to an accretion of complexity and fragmentation to the benefit of nobody.

A number of tensions exist in the current planning system. The certainty versus flexibility debate is often played out in the consideration of adopting a zoning approach (where the plan effectively grants permission) compared with a discretionary system (where the plan leads/guides). The UK has opted to follow the latter path and in doing so needs to accept the inevitability of discussion entering into decision-making. Allied to this are democratic influences in decision-taking and the extent to which experts in their particular field have to play a role.

Planning decisions are taken in a political arena (even if that power is delegated to professional case officers) and the policy direction that frames those decisions is set via central and local government. The friction between the three tiers of governance – national, district, neighbourhood – plays out in town and village halls via devolution of planning powers. The much-heralded community empowerment delivered through neighbourhood planning in England is, in reality, highly constrained by national and district policy. The UK's decision to leave the European Union in March 2019 may result in tension between Westminster and Brussels (the respective seats of power in the UK and the EU).

The extent to which planners can and should be enabling development (as sought under the development management approach), compared with the planning system's role in arbitrating between interests, is perhaps less of a conflict in practice. But it is closely aligned to the contest between private market and public interest, which sits uneasily in a financial climate in which the latter is highly dependent on the former.

When planning the places in which we live, many things need to be considered: public health; environmental implications; trade and economic improvement; governance; access and connectivity; heritage, landscape and the built form; human welfare and socialisation. Therefore, as a final thought, while this chapter has at times painted a rather pessimistic picture of the planning landscape, it is worth reflecting on how the situation might have looked had there been no formal planning structure in place. Would the things we as a society cherish – our landscapes, wildlife, historic places, rural villages, market towns and so on – exist as they do today? Some may consider that planning has been to blame for not curbing the worst excesses of the market. But most would agree, whether for or against development, that if the planning system did not exist we would need to invent something like it, albeit probably not identical to the one we currently operate.

Further reading

Much of the discussion around the latter changes to the planning system has focused on initiatives in England. For greater insight into the planning systems operating in the devolved nations readers are directed to:

Cullingworth, B., Nadin, V., Hart, T., Davoudi, S., Pendlebury, J., Vigar, G., Webb, D. and Townshend, T. (2015) *Town and country planning in the UK* (15th edn), Abingdon, Oxon: Routledge.

A review of history that is more focused on planning law and the planning system can be found in:

Sheppard, A., Peel, D., Richie, H. and Berry, S. (2017) *The essential guide to planning law: Decision-making and practice in the UK*, Bristol: Policy Press.

Notes

[1] By 1991 only two SPZs had been put in place (Ward, 2004: 192).

[2] Introduced through the Local Government Act 1985.

[3] The LDF portfolio included Core Strategy, Local Area Action Plans, site-specific allocations, Proposals Maps and Development Management Policies. There were also 'process' documents that local planning authorities were required to prepare (Statement of Community Involvement, Local Development Scheme).

[4] Hubris: an overestimation of one's abilities.

[5] Ian Dove QC speaking on BBC Radio 4's 'Unreliable Evidence' programme, broadcast 11 April 2012.

4

Governance

Introduction

This chapter explores the governance of planning in the United Kingdom, including the role that organisations and the public play in the process. An understanding of the spatial scales at which planning decisions are made is provided to explain the 'hierarchy' of responsibility on which the planning systems in the UK operate. We outline the different levels at which decisions are made, from the international and national tiers down to district and neighbourhood level, alongside summaries of the agencies of planning, their role and involvement in planning. The diversity agenda is briefly raised before we explore changes in approach to public involvement in the process since the advent of the modern planning system in 1947.

Planning at different scales

The UK has one of the most centralised systems of governance in Europe. Planning in particular has been increasingly guided by legislation and policies set at higher governance levels; therefore, despite a veneer of localism post 2011, decision-making processes and outcomes remain closely steered by the centre. That said, within this framework, each spatial scale in turn sets the context for the decisions and actions taken at lower levels. This 'hierarchy' is fundamental to the operation of our planning system, and a wide range of organisations and institutions contribute to its governance.

At the international scale, there is the:

- **United Nations** (UN, founded in 1945), which is responsible for taking action on a range of major worldwide issues confronting humanity in the 21st century, such as peace and security, climate change, sustainable development, human rights, disarmament, terrorism, humanitarian and health emergencies, gender equality, governance, and food production;[1]
- **United Nations Educational, Scientific and Cultural Organization** (UNESCO, established 1945), which coordinates international cooperation between nations and societies in education, science, communication and culture;[2]
- **Organisation for Economic Co-operation and Development** (OECD, established 1961), which works to promote policies to improve the economic and social wellbeing of people around the world by providing a forum for governments to collaborate on data analysis to predict future trends and to understand what drives economic, social and environmental change;[3]
- **European Union** (EU, came into being in 1999 but was initially established through the creation of the European Communities [EC] in 1951), which is a political and economic union between European countries and is responsible for setting laws that govern how member states operate.[4] In the UK, pre-Brexit, the EU fundamentally influences the strategic arena in which planning takes place, primarily by setting environmental regulations which are then implemented through each member state's legal system. Examples include the Landfill Directive (1999/31/EC), the Water Framework Directive (2000/60/EC) and the Strategic Environmental Assessment Directive (2001/42/EC).

A useful summary of the governance and objectives of the four UK nations can be found on the EU website at: www.special-eu.org/knowledge-pool/module-2-spatial-planning-frameworks/policies-and-objectives/united-kingdom-planning-systems

Central government departments and legislation

The Town and Country Planning Act 1947 established the modern planning system in the UK. Its overarching principles, on which the planning operates, have remained largely unchanged since that time. However, in 1998 'devolution' Acts for Wales, Scotland and Northern Ireland revised the governance hierarchy for each country. While the plan-led approach to planning remains broadly comparable between the four countries, there are now some subtle differences in how the respective planning systems operate (this section should be read in conjunction with Chapters 5 and 6, on the development plan and development management, respectively).

In **England** responsibility for setting the direction and extent of planning processes is held by the Housing, Communities and Local Government department (CLG), headed up by a government minister. Planning policy, against which localised decisions are taken, is set through the National Planning Policy Framework (NPPF). Processes and procedures are regulated through laws written into statutory provisions and decisions on important development proposals are taken as part of ministerial 'called-in' planning applications. The main planning Acts in force are the Town and Country Planning Act 1990 (as amended by the Planning and Compensation Act 1991), the Planning and Compulsory Purchase Act 2004, the Planning Act 2008, the Localism Act 2011, the Growth and Infrastructure Act 2013, and the Planning and Housing Act 2016.

In **Wales** an elected National Assembly was established in 1999. The Government of Wales Act 2006 provided the Assembly with power to introduce legislation on planning, housing, transport, economic development and environmental matters, for example, regulatory 'Orders' such as those for Use Classes and Permitted Development.[5] The main planning Acts are the same as for England, except the Localism Act 2011, which does not apply to Wales. Instead, the Planning (Wales) Act 2015 provides the Assembly with further planning powers.

Scotland has long had a separate judicial and legal system but it was not until 1999 that a directly elected parliament was constituted.[6] It has powers to pass primary legislation, including on planning matters. Planning functions operate under the Town and Country Planning (Scotland) Act 1997, as amended by the Planning etc. (Scotland) Act 2006, and are carried out by the Planning and Architecture Division, which is part of the Directorate for Local Government and Communities.[7] Additionally, heritage planning is covered by the Planning (Listed Buildings and Conservation Areas) (Scotland) Act 1997, as amended by the Historic Environment (Amendment) (Scotland) Act 2011 and the Historic Environment (Scotland) Act 2014.

In **Northern Ireland**, following the Good Friday Agreement of 1998, the Northern Ireland Assembly has responsibility for certain 'transferred' matters, which include planning, housing, transport and economic development.[8] The Planning Act (Northern Ireland) 2011 provides for planning functions to be undertaken by the Department for Infrastructure (DfI) (formerly under the Department of Environment), which is responsible for strategic and regional policy, legislation and determining regionally significant development applications.

A separate but related organisation in England and Wales is the **Planning Inspectorate** (PINS, established in 1992), which is an executive agency of central government/National Assembly Wales and is responsible for handling appeals on refused planning applications; holding inquiries into the preparation of development plans; and nationally significant infrastructure projects (NSIP), on which it reports to the relevant Secretary of State. In Scotland planning appeals are handled by the Planning and Environmental Appeals Division (DPEA) of the Scottish Government. In Northern Ireland the Planning Appeals Commission (PAC) handles planning appeals and reports on examinations into development plans. The commissioners are independent of any government department or agency.

Non-governmental bodies (sometimes referred to as QUANGOs) are statutory bodies responsible for providing specialist advice to local planning authorities on request to assist them in making decisions on proposals:

- In **England** these include the Environment Agency, Historic England, the Homes and Communities Agency, and Natural England.
- In **Wales** heritage is managed by Cadw. Natural Resources Wales took over the work of three bodies: Countryside Council for Wales, Environment Agency Wales, and Forestry Commission Wales.
- In **Scotland** nongovernmental bodies include Scottish Environment Protection Agency, Scottish Natural Heritage, Forestry Commission Scotland, and Historic Environment Scotland.
- In **Northern Ireland** the Historic Environment Division of the Department for Communities looks after heritage matters. The Northern Ireland Environment Agency (NIEA) is an executive agency within the Department of Agriculture, Environment and Rural Affairs and works to protect, conserve and promote the natural environment.

There are also nationally based non-statutory interest groups that put forward their specialist opinions on issues of particular interest to their membership. Examples of organisations include the Ramblers (formerly the Ramblers' Association), the Royal Society for the Protection of Birds (RSPB), Friends of the Earth, the Campaign to Protect Rural England (CPRE), the Country Land and Business Association (CLA), and the National Trust.

At the regional scale:

- **Regional Assemblies** (created in England in 1998 and abolished in 2010) acted as regional planning bodies that prepared a Regional Spatial Strategy, which replaced the strategic planning (structure plan) function of English county councils. This regional tier was comprised of indirectly elected members from local authorities and other interests in their region. The regional tier was removed in 2010 and replaced with a 'duty-to-cooperate' between local authorities, in recognition of the need to plan for a larger-than-local scale. The only regional tier remaining in England is the Greater London Authority.

- **Regional Development Agencies** (RDAs, created in 1998 and abolished in 2012) were non-departmental public bodies that operated across nine English 'regions' prior to their removal in March 2012. Their primary role was to drive and coordinate economic development in their respective regions and to reduce imbalances between regions.
- **Local Economic Partnerships** (LEPs, first established in 2011) are business-led partnerships between local authorities and businesses in England. In 2017 there were 39 LEPs in England operating at a sub-regional level (groups of local authority areas) to pursue initiatives that drive economic growth within their functional area.[9]

At county/district level:

- In **England** in 2018 there are 353 local authorities (also referred to as local government, or local councils).[10] These comprise two main formats: two-tier authorities, with a county council and multiple district councils sharing planning responsibilities (often the 'shire' counties of England); and unitary authorities taking on all of the planning functions for a smaller but more populated area (usually city-based metropolitan urban areas such as Greater Manchester). The council responsible for carrying out planning functions is called the local planning authority (LPA).
- In **Scotland** there are 32 councils and 2 national park authorities,[11] and in **Wales** there are 22 county/borough councils,[12] which have 'all-purpose' planning powers equivalent to the unitary authorities of England. In **Northern Ireland** there are 11 district/borough/city councils with responsibility for preparing a development plan, determining 'local' planning applications and enforcement.[13]
- **National Park Authorities** operate in National Park areas and have LPA planning responsibilities.
- **Development Corporations** were created in some locations to either take over local planning powers, such as the Thames

Gateway Urban Development Corporation, or to coordinate regeneration development between public and private bodies, such as Gloucester Heritage Urban Regeneration Company.

At the neighbourhood level:

• **Parish and town councils** are the lowest tier of elected representation in England. They have a formal opportunity to comment on planning applications prior to them being determined by the higher-tier local planning authorities. The Localism Act 2011 (England) has now also given them the option to prepare a neighbourhood development plan and community right to build orders. In non-parished places, such as many metropolitan areas, a neighbourhood forum can be constituted to carry out the neighbourhood planning function.[14] This power does not exist in the devolved nations.

Integration between tiers of governance

The extent to which organisations and their objectives are 'joined up', both internally and externally, can be fundamental to the success, or otherwise, of a particular policy or strategy they are pursuing. The concept of integration between tiers/locations can be considered through the notion of three 'directions' (Nadin and Seaton, 2006):

• **Horizontal:** between agencies that operate in the same location but with different remits for the same issue. For example, a district/borough council, a county council and the Environment Agency will all have responsibilities for dealing with flooding issues in a particular location but the level of integration between the approaches each takes can be instrumental in determining the success of any joint action taken. This integration can also be internal within an organisation, for example, between different local authority departments such as Housing and Building Control, which will have their own minimum standards for residential accommodation. In this context it is sometimes referred to as overcoming compartmentalisation or silo working.

- **Vertical:** between tiers of government at different spatial scales. An example of this would be the way that policies cascade down from central government (for example, the NPPF in England or the NPF in Scotland, or Planning Policy Wales in Wales), through local government (in their local plan), down to parish/town councils who have to 'generally conform' to the content in their neighbourhood plans. The principle of subsidiarity is that power should rest with the lowest level of governance for which it is practical to administer.
- **Territorial:** between bodies in different geographical locations with different political administrations, such as adjacent local authorities, where there is a common issue. Examples would include housing market areas, flood risk management and river catchments, transport corridors, and economic growth.

This model can help us to understand and explain the linkages and relationships between and across tiers of governance. Where there is divergence in approach between dimensions and directions then this can cause tensions between the parties involved, which may lead to conflict and ineffective implementation.

Added to this directional dimension is that of 'intensity' of integration between both the bodies themselves and the policies/objectives they seek to implement.[15] This relates to the extent to which organisations are connected, from loose associations and informal networks at one end to seamless joined-up partnership working at the other, where all parties share joint responsibility for decision-making and the outcomes.

As well as organisations, there are also many actors involved in planning processes. Another aspect to consider, therefore, is the way in which stakeholders, including the public, are integrated into the planning process and the intensity with which that occurs. Public involvement in planning processes is sometimes referred to a 'double-edged sword': while it can add delay and difficulties to the process, it can also curb the worst excesses of comprehensive redevelopment that, in its totality, destroys the heritage (and other interests) that we have now come to cherish (Burke, 1975). The plurality of interests necessitates working relationships between the professional planner (with expertise), the elected councillors (who make the decisions), the developer/landowner (who puts forward and implements the proposals), the technical specialists (who provide subject-specific expertise), and the public (whose interests are supposed to be being planned for).

Public involvement in planning

A landowner's right to develop their land as they see fit was replaced in 1947 by public control over the development and use of land in the 'public interest'. Planning for the public interest necessarily requires political intervention in unfettered free-market activity, which in turn is influenced by politicians' perceptions of public demands.

There are two main strands to planning: the *process* (what happens when and how) and the *content* (the policy or proposal being discussed). When people get involved in planning issues it tends to be as a consequence of their interest in the latter, yet it is through the former that the potential for timely and meaningful involvement occurs. While some people participate in planning processes from a principled or moral stance, for example, opposition to a nuclear power station proposal regardless of whether it affects them directly or not, there are others whose involvement is motivated by perceived personal impact, often not extending beyond their own narrowly derived interests. In order to effectively communicate one's views on the content, it is necessary to understand the process in which this legally needs to occur. This process–content debate is raised throughout the chapter.

Defining public interest, community, diversity and participation

The terms 'public' and 'community' are often used interchangeably, but a vocal minority of local residents may not be representative of wider public interest or opinion. Planning decisions that are made in favour of development where there have been public objections is sometimes labelled as 'undemocratic', despite the decision makers having been elected by the wider local residents to make such decisions on their behalf. The remoteness of the bureaucracy is sometimes seen as being a factor in reinforcing such a view.

In the context of planning, *community* is usually taken to mean those people living within a particular neighbourhood or locality. Communities in reality are comprised of a diverse array of people who do not necessarily live in spatially juxtaposed accommodation. Diversity incorporates many different equality issues, such as gender, ethnicity, age, class, disability, sex, culture and religion. Often people sharing certain traits are categorised together as 'minority' groups and treated as peripheral to the 'average man in the street' (Greed and Johnson, 2014: 296). But, given that women comprise over half of the UK population, this means that the lack of awareness of the needs of such groups has ironically resulted in planning being implemented for the few rather than for the many.

In the media, community is often characterised as a small group of local residents, usually middle-aged, standing outside their local council offices or next to a green field proposed for development holding placards with their group's name forming a catchy acronym. If protesters' views are not acceded to there often follows a cry that the elected councillors' decision is 'undemocratic'. However, the representativeness of these more vocal and active people for wider public opinion is rarely questioned, yet their involvement, and their right to participate in the process, is taken for granted. It was not always so, as the historical context section below explains.

Public participation in development processes is a 'powerful concept', but also one full of 'ambiguities', which belies its seemingly obvious meaning. Despite this, it has become a panacea without which any respectable project is incomplete (Michener, 1998: 2105). Specifically in relation to the planning process, public participation involves 'doing as well as talking', requiring 'active' involvement in the process (Skeffington, 1969, in Dennis, 1972: 220). Figure 4.1 illustrates how key terminology around public participation can be viewed as a continuum, from passive informing to active partnership.

Figure 4.1: The terminology of participation viewed as a continuum

Passive → Active

Informing   Consultation   Involvement   Participation   Collaboration   Partnership

Informing: a one-way flow of information to provide interested parties with sufficient knowledge so that they understand what is happening but there is no formal mechanism for dialogue between parties. This is a passive approach to 'consultation'.

Consultation: a two-way flow of information in which opinions are sought and considered but decision makers are not obliged to implement comments received. While this is more active than merely informing people, it is still a predominantly passive activity.

Involvement: a more proactive approach to 'consultation' in which participants can contribute to the process if they wish.

Participation: an active involvement in decision-making requiring a dialogue between parties and contributions towards decision-making.

Collaboration: an active involvement in developing solutions and directly influencing decisions. This usually involves in-depth working relationships although one party is usually a more dominant (leading) participant.

Partnership: this requires coproduction of solutions involving joint working and joint responsibility for the outcomes. Both parties are equally accountable for benefits and liabilities that occur.

The historical context for public participation in planning in England

When the UK's modern planning system was conceived in the 1940s there was very little public involvement in planning decision-making processes. Indeed, the public were actively discouraged from taking part, as it was considered that technocrats who were qualified to make such calculated judgements knew what was best for people and would act in their best interests. This approach belied the social and environmental impacts of development and led to a rise in public protest, which was also prevalent in other countries at the time (most notably the United States). The decades that followed have seen a steady but inexorable increase in public involvement, albeit with rather minimal consultation requirements compared with the current 'coproduction' approach under the Localism Act 2011.

Public participation in UK planning in the modern era can be grouped into seven progressive periods,[16] which broadly follow the decades:

1. The immediate postwar (Second World War) experience in the 1950s following creation of the modern planning system
2. The mid–late 1960s, with a rise in public protest
3. Increased public participation in the 1970s
4. A drive for market efficiency in the 1980s
5. The rise of 'stakeholder' participation and service delivery efficiency during the 1990s
6. The spatial planning approach, with Statements of Community Involvement (SCIs), in the 2000s
7. The post-2010 localism agenda devolving planning powers to neighbourhoods.

Participation post war and in the 1950s

The modern planning system operating in England, as instigated by the Town and Country Planning Act 1947, did not encourage public participation, 'even to the extent of denying information about planning proposals in their formative stages' (Ward, 2004: 123). There was a belief during the post-war era of planning in the status of 'experts': that they should be trusted to make the right decisions, and thus that public participation had little role in making planning decisions. Planning was consequently seen as a 'disabling' profession. The growth of professionals, on whom public trust rested, 'to address the physical spatial development problems of the nation' was in effect a 'depoliticisation' of an activity which is inherently political and was 'later appreciated to be of intense public concern' (Cullingworth and Nadin, 2006: 432).

Public concern about the planning process led to a recommendation to open up planning inquiries to the public,[17] as this was 'the forum in which a much greater degree of public participation can take place' (McAuslan, 1980: 47). This shifted the role of the local authority in the planning process from one that acted on behalf of the public in arbitrating between public and private interests to one in which public participation was introduced into the relationship (Booth, 2003: 118). The notion of 'advocacy' planning derived from experiences in 1950s/'60s America, where it was felt that 'the voice of the poor did not get represented in the planning process' (Damer and Hague, 1971: 218). Advocacy planning adopted an approach whereby alternative community-led plans would be prepared in contrast to a public agency's plan, with the planner acting as an advocate of the public, responding as an agent would to a client (Davidoff, 1965: 425). In comparison to the preparation of development plans, the process of determining planning applications was largely unacknowledged during the 1950s. In part this was due to the betterment taxation system that was in place in the early part of the decade, which resulted in some developers concealing their intentions to avoid paying market prices for property (Booth, 2003: 108; Ward, 2004: 115). To overcome such issues the Town and Country Planning Act 1959 introduced measures to 'improve the quality of information given to the public ... about planning applications' (Ward, 2004: 115). The theme of access to information is an important one if those that wish to engage in the process are to play a meaningful part.

Power and participation in the 1960s

Public participation in planning was first mentioned in professional planning literature in 1964 (Jackson, 1964: 6; see also the editorial in the same issue). At this time there was growing public disaffection with the quality of new development (Rydin, 1999: 185) and more fundamentally with the way power was managed and distributed across society (Ward, 2004: 123; Cullingworth et al, 2015: 509). The rise of civil rights movements in America had the effect of 'motivating people to ask "Why?" more often' (Damer and Hague, 1971: 219). In England this led to a number of central government policy initiatives, including a 1967 study commissioned by the Ministry of Housing and Local Government to examine the way that local authorities were discharging their development control functions and carrying out consultation arrangements 'fairly, openly and impartially' (Booth, 2003: 121).

During the 1960s the notion of participatory democracy (in the form of public participation in the planning process), as opposed to representative democracy (decisions made by elected members), was seen as way of providing checks and balances on the operation of a system that was not subject to central government control (Ward, 2004: 123). At this time 'the idea of an objective, neutral planning system was increasingly challenged' due to the failures in addressing social and economic decline (Cullingworth and Nadin, 2006: 432) and Rydin (1999: 195) notes that discussions on participation identified 'a profound distrust of planners in the way that they relate to the public'.

While public participation was 'seen as a good thing in its own right' (Rydin, 1999: 186) it was also considered an 'administrative necessity if the whole British planning system was not to disintegrate' (Damer and Hague, 1971: 221). One of the main reasons for this was the increasing concerns of those directly affected by slum clearance (that is, the people being dispossessed) as well as the more affluent and articulate home owners on the urban/rural fringe where the new estates were to be built (Damer and Hague, 1971: 222). Increasing public participation was seen as a means of increasing public acceptability of schemes and the Labour government established the Skeffington Committee to examine methods for securing public participation in planning processes. The resultant report (Skeffington, 1969) represents a watershed in the consideration of public involvement in planning processes. It refers to the public needing to better understand the notion of planning in order to fully understand the proposals before them (para 193) as a 'pre-requisite of [providing] informed comment and discussion' (para 249).

In response to 'top-down' city renewal slum clearance programmes in the United States, Sherry Arnstein published her 'Ladder of Citizen Participation' (1969). Her model intimated at people climbing the rungs of a ladder to rise from experiencing *manipulation* at the bottom towards gaining *citizen control* at the top. There are eight 'rungs': Manipulation, Therapy, Informing, Consultation, Placation, Partnership, Delegated Power and Citizen Control (the diagram in Figure 4.2 maps these stages against the changes in public participation experienced in the UK since the 1940s; see pages 89 and 90). The 'rungs' are divided into three broad categories: the first two rungs comprising 'non-participation'; the next three being 'tokenism'; and the top three reflecting degrees of 'citizen power' (Arnstein, 1969).

This model is sometimes presented as a 'wheel of participation' (Davidson, 1998) to address criticism of the implication that climbing up the rungs to attain citizen control is the most desirable outcome in every instance. It is also sometimes represented as a 'scaffold' to emphasise the three-dimensional aspects of participation where multiple groups and interests are involved and participation is dynamic and evolutionary, with diverse users requiring different methods and levels of participation (Tritter and McCallum, 2006: 164). An additional factor to consider is the intensity of participation, referring to the depth, vigour, quality and longevity of involvement.

A particularly interesting comment in the Skeffington Report is in its consideration of the notion of 'community'. The report states that:

> We do not think of the public solely in terms of the community as it shows itself in organised groups. We regard the community

as an aggregate comprising all the individuals and groups within it without limitation. (Skeffington, 1969: para 5)

The importance of this is summed up by Dennis (1972: 230), who notes that this effectively allows the local planning authority to 'override the views of any specific individual or group in the name of the wishes whether expressed or not of any other individual or group'. It raises an important point in defining who comprises 'the community' in any given instance and the inappropriateness of assuming that any one group, or individual, speaks on behalf of wider interests.

A significant weakness of Skeffington's report was that it focused on methods for letting the public know about the technical 'structural' aspects of the process rather than considering in any detail what 'participation ought to achieve' beyond reducing the number of objections in order to speed up the determination process (Dennis, 1972: 224). Unfortunately, Skeffington's report was therefore not the landmark it should have been, with its recommendations 'mundane and rather obvious' (Cullingworth and Nadin, 2006: 432) and 'disappointing and cautious' (Ward, 2004: 123). It did not explore the issue of shifting power away from the local planning authority (elected members and planners) to the community (the electorate). A further weakness of the report was that it was written with the implicit assumption that planning was an apolitical activity where the only source of conflict in the process would be derived from the public's 'ignorance of planning matters', which could be overcome by educating people through participation assisted by supportive media coverage (Damer and Hague, 1971: 223). This reoccurring theme of educating the public to understand the planners' perspective appears to have more in common with a social marketing approach than genuine participation. Skeffington's suggested approach could therefore be likened to a public relations exercise for the planning profession (Damer and Hague, 1971: 224). The nature of the pluralistic society in which the English planning system operates means that there is usually a diversity of interests with often competing values. Davidoff (1965: 431) argued that it was therefore planners themselves that required education.

Although Skeffington's report 'stimulated considerable debate' (Damer and Hague, 1971: 217) many of the recommendations were 'watered down' in implementation, for example, the creation of community forums proving little more than an information conduit between the local planning authority and community groups in order to place a tick in the consultation box (Rydin, 1999: 187). While the Skeffington Report essentially covers 'how to do' public participation, it was the Town and Country Planning Act 1968 that laid the statutory foundations for involvement.

Expanded participation in the 1970s

A main debate in the 1970s was the extent to which planning processes were causing delay in delivering development. Involving the community was therefore relegated to the background (Booth, 2003: 132) and local authority consultation/publicity duties were 'carefully limited and phrased' in statutory documentation (McAuslan, 1980: 14). Department of the Environment Circular 71/73 allowed locally elected councils to administer the system as they deemed appropriate, such that the local authority was both the determinant of the application and also the arbiter of the extent to which the proposal was publicised.

The Dobry Report (Dobry, 1975) undertook extensive analysis of the development control process, including the 'mechanics of public consultation', and at the time it was the most 'comprehensive ... ever attempted' (Booth, 2003: 123, 130). In respect of participation, it made some important statements:

> The proper function of public involvement should be clearly understood and not exceeded. It should assist elected members and central government by giving them information and other help they may need, but should not impinge on their prerogative of decision-making. (Dobry, 1975: para 10.6)

However, the report goes on to state:

> Planners should be aware of ignoring or making assumptions
> about the attitudes of neighbourhoods which ordinarily display
> little interest in civic affairs. They must not write off the non-
> joiners ... These people have a right to be consulted. (Dobry,
> 1975: para 10.40)

Interestingly, the report then defines some of the terminology used
as follows:

> The process needs to be in effect 'participation' (which means
> taking an active part, from the outset, in the formulation of
> ... decisions of strategic importance) rather than 'consultation'
> (which means giving the public an opportunity to express views
> on planning applications). (Dobry, 1975: para 10.47)

The Dobry Report, however, was largely ignored by the Labour
government of the time who considered, in their belated response,
that the balance between 'the right of the public to be informed
about proposed development in their area and the burden ... on
applicants and local authorities is about right' (DoE Circular 113/75,
in McAuslan, 1980: 17). Shortly after Dobry's report was published,
the government undertook its own study focusing in particular
on inefficiency and delay, predicated on an essentially anecdotal
belief that the planning system was becoming 'bogged down in
bureaucratic processes' (House of Commons, 1977, vol 2: 47, in
Booth, 2003: 128).

Efficiency in the 1980s

The newly elected Conservative government under Margaret
Thatcher (4 May 1979 to 28 November 1990) initially saw the
planning system as a tool for assisting the market in delivering
development. The creation of Urban Development Corporations
that had their own planning powers to drive regeneration,
effectively bypassing local planning authorities, exemplifies a
central government approach that distrusted local decision-making.

These corporations, whose aim was 'to get things done and not get diverted by consultation ... may prove to be the last major, full scale manifestation of a kind of "traditional" urban policy based upon physical planning which effectively excluded the wider community' (Shaw and Robinson, 2010: 125). They were successful in regenerating large areas of derelict and contaminated land within cities, but there were concerns over the extent to which existing industry was merely being relocated, as opposed to creating new opportunities and benefiting wider objectives (Cullingworth et al, 2015: 448).

The Secretary of State, Nicholas Ridley, presented the argument that 'in the interests of the country as a whole, local concerns need to be set aside in favour of a presumption in favour of new development' (Cullingworth et al, 2015: 511). This perpetuates the impression of a system 'weighted firmly in favour of the development industry and not the public at large' (Booth, 2003: 133). The intense backlash that this caused from the conservative element of the Conservative electorate in the late 1980s resulted in a volte-face under the politicised banner of providing 'local choice', though in reality central government retained control by requiring local planning authorities to operate within confines set out in planning policy guidance notes (Cullingworth et al, 2015: 511).

The term NIMBY ('Not In My Back Yard') was popularised in the UK in the 1980s. It is now frequently used as a pejorative term to denounce opponents to development. The rise of the NIMBY has gone hand in hand with approaches to increase public involvement in planning processes, which can be seen as either providing a platform from which people can air their personal opinions or, conversely, as a way of diluting the most extreme opinions by providing an opportunity for the majority of previously unheard voices to be vocalised. Opposition to planning applications tends to be motivated either by an objection to the specifics of the proposal – for example, its design, siting, access, visual impact, amenity or incompatibility with neighbouring land uses – or an objection to the principle of the development – that is, the proposal is for something that would be objected to regardless of its location – for example, a waste incinerator, fracking for shale gas or a nuclear power station. These two motivations are not mutually exclusive and those concerned about the former often draw on arguments derived from the latter to add weight to their position.

By way of contrast, a 'classic example of popular planning' at the time is the Coin Street redevelopment in London. where, following protracted inquiries and legal wrangling, a community scheme was finally developed in which the community's role went beyond that of a 'consultative' body; rather, it was an active participant in the process (Brindley et al, 1996: 90). The Coin Street community activists demonstrated a sophisticated 'horses for courses' approach that exhibited formality/informality and participation/opposition as appropriate for the situation at any given time (Brindley et al, 1996: 91). This case is distinct in that the local authority sided with the community, in contrast to other schemes in the vicinity in which the local council had 'encouraged' developers to proceed with proposals on the basis of local authority-adopted strategies prepared without public consultation (Booth, 2003: 131).

The rise of the citizen as a stakeholder in the 1990s

The belief that service quality could be driven through creation of Citizen's Charters emerged during the early 1990s under John Major's Conservative government. This approach saw the public as customers of a service, characterised by greater public scrutiny of the services they were receiving. Aside from the appropriateness of relaying reciprocation of individuals' taxes for receipt of public services, and developers directly paying for their planning applications to be determined, there is the wider matter of whether a service such as planning, operating in the public interest, can and should deliver on an individual's demands.

Cullingworth and Nadin (2006: 435) note that some local authority planning services enthusiastically took up the opportunity to issue their own Planning Charters; however, in doing so they generally just reiterated existing service requirements rather than extending the rights of the public to engage in the planning process. While such charters were limited in one sense, they did present the public with an opportunity to better understand the process as it existed, and in that arena were 'welcomed' (Cullingworth and Nadin, 2006: 435). Other authorities entered into 'planning for real' exercises with their populations in order to 'build strong community networks ... [as a mechanism] through which the public would participate' (Rydin, 1999: 193). Assumptions were made normatively about values, aspirations and interests based upon a person's geographic place of residence, which did not always relate to the 'sense of community as experienced by residents' (Rydin, 1999: 193).

As the 1990s progressed, and Tony Blair's New Labour government was elected in 1997, there was a shift from the language of *consumers* to *communities*, and in turn to *stakeholders*. The requirement for local authorities to prepare 'community strategies' presented a new mechanism for improving wider involvement in policy (Cullingworth et al, 2015: 511). The introduction of stakeholder terminology implied an elevated status for those participating in planning processes. However, the empowerment that this status implied was tempered by an audit culture in local authorities,[18] which meant that local authorities (and local planning authorities in particular) were constantly wary of criticism and rigidly followed identified procedures to avoid legal action (Rydin, 1999: 195). In terms of public involvement, this recourse to the participation rule book meant that standard operating practices were rolled out for each case rather than bespoke solutions being tailored to specific communities and their circumstances. Such bureaucracy inevitably favours those communities switched on to institutional mechanisms, but in turn can disadvantage peripheral groups such as ethnic minorities (Thomas and Krishnarayan, 1994: 1899, in Rydin, 1999: 194).

The desire to achieve consensus rather than getting bogged down in conflict, and the recognition of diversity within society, reflected a more communicative and collaborative approach to planning (Healey, 1997). The outcome, rather unsurprisingly, was that more than one 'right answer' could be argued, which ironically presented increased opportunity for conflict to arise between stakeholder groups and brought to the fore difficulties of representativeness and in the ability of planners to arbitrate between such interests (Greed and Johnson, 2014: 160).

Sustainable communities in the 2000s

Critics of planning have understandably often focused their attention on the determination of planning applications, as this is the 'sharp end' of the development process and is frequently in the local media spotlight. In citing inefficient and reactive practices as being significant weaknesses, the critique focused on the *process* element of the activity, with little reference to the planning system's *content* (that is, what planning seeks to achieve). In order to address these criticisms, in the new millennium New Labour instigated what it saw as 'fundamental reform' (DTLR, 2001) of the planning system, culminating in the Planning Act 2004, which was 'promised to be more transparent and inclusive than ever before in its dealings with local communities' (Ward, 2004: 241). The introduction of Statements of Community Involvement (SCI) to set out the local planning authority approach to public participation, and front-loaded participation at the initial stages of plan preparation, were key components of this (Cullingworth et al, 2015: 512). This presented a shift from consultation *post* event (once a scheme had been designed) to a proactive, shaping role *prior* to the final preparation (Curry, 2012: 350).

Ward (2004: 242) notes that part of these reforms was 'encouragement' for greater community involvement in planning applications, with 'funds for expert planning aid ... easier access to planning documents and greater transparency'. While on the face of it this may seem like an appropriate approach, there is a concern that a community's reliance on support from government-funded institutions, or organisations from within the bureaucracy (for example, the planners working for the local planning authority), effectively institutionalises the community representatives, rendering them 'unable to take an independent critical line' (Brindley et al, 1996: 90).

Localism in 2010 and beyond

The UK Coalition government formed in May 2010 promised a community-led localist approach to planning. The Localism Act 2011 confirmed these intentions by legislating for parish/town councils and neighbourhood forums in England to prepare legally binding development plans, set out community rights to build and provide community powers of decision-making. Localism, however, is not a new concept, having been identified in the 1990s as an approach in which a small number of locally successful projects are heralded as comprising a panacea for wider regional and national action (Lovering, 1995). 'With every new government for the past 20 years proclaiming its supposed allegiance to greater local empowerment and repudiation of past centralist approaches, it is hard not to be sceptical about the current claims that are being made about radical changes in approach' (Haughton and Allmendinger, 2012: 2). This is especially so when combined with the pro-growth agenda being championed by the government at the time. 'Planning is situated at the critical junction between the Coalition Government's "Big Society" and localism agendas on the one hand, and the growth agenda on the other; a burden that is likely to prove heavy for the circumscribed activity that is contemporary land-use and spatial planning in the UK' (Valler et al, 2012: 459).

The Localism Act 2011 also requires proposers of large-scale development schemes to proactively engage with 'communities' (however so defined – which is a matter of much debate).[19] The proposed scheme needs to be far enough advanced to present something meaningful and tangible to interested parties, but not so complete that it offers little in the way of potential for amendment. The stage at which a planning application is submitted falls towards the implementation end of the process rather than at the conceptual stage, and is therefore too late in the day to undertake meaningful engagement.

The Localism Act 2011 places neighbourhood plans, which have their origins in non-statutory village design statements and parish plans, on a formal statutory footing with full development plan status on adoption. The take-up of neighbourhood planning has been strong in affluent rural areas, where pressure for new housing has stimulated residents to engage more proactively in the planning process. While the government has been clear in its statements that neighbourhood plans cannot be used as a mechanism to resist development,[20] this has not dissuaded many parishes from trying. By March 2018 there had been over 2,500 areas designated for neighbourhood planning and 542 plans formally adopted, or 'made' (Lichfields, 2018). Preparing a neighbourhood plan is not cheap, the average cost being around £13,000 (Planning Aid, undated), although some have cost substantially more. It is not just the monetary cost involved; there is also the time commitment required (over two years in most cases) and the expertise necessary to understand the regulatory and policy aspects. The limited number of plans coming forward in more deprived areas, combined with the withdrawal of funding for urban regeneration, has led to concerns that the localist agenda is 'socially regressive' (Cullingworth et al, 2015: 513).

Neighbourhood planning on the face of it places greater planning powers in the hands of communities than ever before. But the extent of citizen power is (severely) constrained by the hierarchy of plans and policies that provide the context in which neighbourhood plans must be prepared. While qualifying bodies will set the agenda and vision for their defined area, the local planning authority will be involved as the neighbourhood plan progresses and, along with an independent examiner, will serve to temper the content such that the initial intent can be lost (or at least obscured). See, for example, the case of Swanwick Neighbourhood Plan (Derbyshire, October 2016), where their submitted plan changed so much following examination that the qualifying body actively, and successfully, campaigned for a 'no' vote at referendum so that it could not be formally made/adopted. The neighbourhood planning approach could therefore be seen as one of coproduction rather than a solely bottom-up endeavour. There are also questions as to the extent to which 'community' in this context is being used as an instrument to deliver centrally predetermined outcomes, the most obvious being the provision of housing (Brownhill and Bradley, 2017).

Perspectives: theory, rhetoric and reality

Figure 4.2 shows the change in public involvement in planning processes indicatively mapped against the eight steps on Arnstein's theoretical ladder. By inserting key legislation, policy, theories and events into the chart we can build up a picture of change over time and the influences and responses that have shaped our approach to people's involvement in the planning system. What is noticeable from including the political context in the graph is that advances in public involvement have occurred during both Labour (centre left) and Conservative (right of centre) led administrations.

Negotiation in the planning system

The development of land encompasses a plurality of interests, including those of the landowner, neighbouring residents, interest groups, businesses, statutory consultees and the local authority (incorporating locally elected members). This necessitates parties coming together to seek solutions. Negotiation is therefore fundamental to the successful performance of any discretionary planning system like that operating in the UK.

Positional negotiation and *principled* bargaining are two different strategies: the former comprises a situation in which the negotiator seeks the best outcome for their situation (assuming a zero-sum game), while the latter involves attaining greater understanding of another party's positions/interests in order to derive mutually beneficial solutions (Claydon, 1999: 110; Claydon and Chick, 2005: 223). Information and knowledge are critical when participating in planning processes: 'Information is power' (Cullingworth and Nadin, 2006: 451), and 'whoever controls knowledge controls everything' (Dennis, 1972: 167). 'Although knowledge is not in itself a guarantee of power a critic who can be deprived of the facts, or even better fed with misinformation, will surely be powerless' (Dennis, 1972: 167). The level of knowledge and understanding a community possesses will significantly influence the success of their involvement (Curry, 2012: 353). 'The extent to which communities actually have such

Figure 4.2: Participation 'steps' in planning processes indicatively mapped against Arnstein's ladder

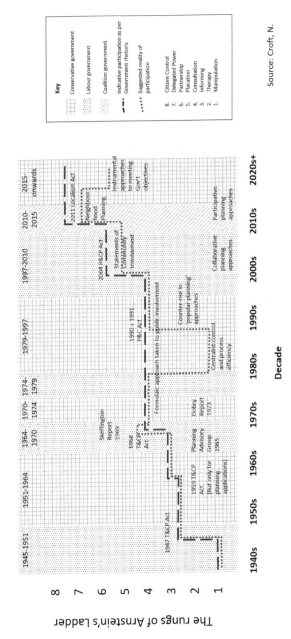

Source: Croft, N.

Source: Croft, N.

knowledge will influence the quality of the outcomes of the decisions with which they are involved. The extent to which they are perceived to have such knowledge (by planning professionals) will influence the process of decision making' (Curry, 2012: 353).

The earlier in the planning process negotiation is undertaken, the greater the chance of influence being exerted effectively over the proposals. Case officers, the local authority officers with responsibility for working on the application, hold considerable power in this respect, acting as regulators of the knowledge available to different parties (Sheppard et al, 2015). They also have power to exercise their discretion in operationalising opportunities that may become apparent as part of considering any given proposal, with professional knowledge and expertise, along with personal judgement and values coming into play. The attitude of the case officer is therefore a 'key component' in the approach to negotiating that is followed (Claydon and Chick, 2005: 225). The extent to which planners can be considered the 'guardians' of the public interest (Damer and Hague, 1971: 225) is reflected in their role as the 'gatekeepers to planning permission' (Coulson, 2003: 182). The complicated nature of the planning process means that planners are very much 'in the driving seat' as they negotiate between parties and subsequently make recommendations to the decision taker (Coulson, 2003: 183).

Conclusions

This chapter has outlined the governance bodies that administer and deliver planning functions in the UK. At the time of writing this book the impact of the UK's exit from the European Union (set for March 2019) is far from certain, but it is likely to involve considerable changes in the higher tiers of legislative administration and policy making. However, the impacts at the neighbourhood level, as far as planning is concerned, are likely to be masked by the already heavily centralised operation of the planning system in England in particular.

Public participation in planning processes is now considered a basic 'right', but it was not always so. The system was predicated on the assumption that planning professionals were the experts best placed to deliver what was in the public interest. As the 20th century progressed, calls for reform resulted in increased involvement of the public in planning. More recently, the Planning and Compulsory Purchase Act 2004 and the Localism Act 2011 have placed further emphasis on, and have arguably created greater opportunities for, increased public involvement in planning (Sheppard et al, 2015). The rise of community planning through neighbourhood plans in particular has placed an expectation on communities to be actively involved in designing and delivering desired outcomes. However, despite this, questions remain concerning the effectiveness of public participation in planning decision-making (Cullingworth et al, 2015).

It is also questionable whether the localist planning agenda in England, whereby majority referendum is required to pass/reject schemes, will create a scenario in which planning becomes a 'tyranny of the masses', where the majority rule at the expense or even oppression of minority views/interests (noting that the majority may actually be wrong). In such circumstances questions remain as to who speaks on behalf of the underrepresented, disadvantaged or other interests (for example, ecological, heritage or environmental designations) that do not have a 'voice' in the traditional sense (instead, they have an abstract 'policy' or regulatory voice), and also how such 'voices' are represented in a referendum vote.

There is a tendency for proponents of public participation to espouse the benefits of community empowerment. However, this needs to be tempered against low levels of community participation by groups who are not strongly in favour of or against a particular scheme, and decision-making by 'the local community' will therefore almost inevitably be skewed towards the wants of a subset of that community without recourse to wider societal benefits (Rydin, 1999: 195). The evolution of public participation in the planning process has resulted in a system that favours well-organised 'minor elites' (small groups), giving them a 'relatively privileged position' despite them often being no more 'representative of anything wider than the interests of their active supporters' (Cullingworth and Nadin, 2006: 447). 'Planning purely by the local community can be justified only if no other claims on that local space are recognised' (Rydin, 1999: 196).

Further reading

For more information on neighbourhood planning, you are directed to the online resources of Locality (https://locality.org.uk) and Planning Aid (https://www.rtpi.org.uk/planning-aid). An interesting discussion about how neighbourhood planning has shaped up after its first five years is offered in:

Brownhill, S. and Bradley, Q. (2017) *Localism and neighbourhood planning: Power to the people?*, Bristol: Policy Press.

For a more comprehensive discussion around diversity and equality issues, you should read Chapter 15 of:

Greed, C. and Johnson, D. (2014) *Planning in the UK: An introduction*, London: Palgrave Macmillan.

A broader and more detailed consideration of governance issues in general can be found in:

Cullingworth, B., Nadin, V., Hart, T., Davoudi, S., Pendlebury, J., Vigar, G., Webb, D. and Townshend, T. (2015) *Town and country planning in the UK* (15th edn), Abingdon, Oxon: Routledge.

Notes

[1] www.un.org/en/sections/about-un/overview
[2] http://en.unesco.org/about-us/introducing-unesco
[3] www.oecd.org/about
[4] https://europa.eu/european-union/index_en
[5] https://www.gov.uk/guidance/devolution-settlement-wales
[6] https://www.gov.uk/guidance/devolution-settlement-scotland
[7] www.gov.scot/Topics/Built-Environment/planning/Roles/Scottish-Government
[8] https://www.gov.uk/guidance/devolution-settlement-northern-ireland
[9] www.lepnetwork.net/about-us

10 https://www.gov.uk/guidance/local-government-structure-and-elections

11 www.gov.scot/Topics/Government/local-government/localg/usefullinks

12 http://wlga.wales/welsh-local-authority-links

13 https://www.nidirect.gov.uk/contacts/local-councils-in-northern-ireland

14 A neighbourhood forum must comprise 21 persons who live in, or have an interest in the area, and be broadly representative of the electorate and business interests.

15 For a more detailed discussion on integration and joined-up working you are directed to the briefing note article 'The idea of policy integration and spatial planning' (Nadin and Seaton, 2006).

16 The first five periods are identified in Rydin (1999: 184); the latter two are added by the authors.

17 The recommendation of the Franks Committee on Administrative Tribunals and Enquiries (1957).

18 This was driven by the Nolan Committee's 'Standards in Public Life' call for probity in public bodies.

19 Major planning applications are those for residential developments of 200+ dwellings (or with site areas of 4+ hectares) or commercial developments with a floor space of 10,000+ square metres (or with a site area of 2+ hectares).

20 Planning Practice Guidance for Neighbourhood Planning (August 2017, para 43) states that: 'The resulting draft neighbourhood plan must meet the basic conditions if it is to proceed. National planning policy states that it should support the strategic development needs set out in the Local Plan, plan positively to support local development and should not promote less development than set out in the Local Plan or undermine its strategic policies (see paragraph 16 and paragraph 184 of the National Planning Policy Framework). Nor should it be used to constrain the delivery of a strategic site allocated for development in the Local Plan.' Available at: https://www.gov.uk/guidance

5

Plans and policy: looking forward

Introduction

This chapter introduces the role of plans and policy in the making and management of place and space. It refers to some of the key components of a typical plan and outlines some key plan-making principles, such as the need for an effective evidence base and proactive community and stakeholder involvement. The chapter introduces the concept of the UK's plan-led system and the role of the statutory development plan. It introduces key policy goals and outlines some of the plan-making activities that planners need to engage with.

Defining a plan

Whatever role a planner has, it is likely that they will interact with some kind of plan. If they work in the public sector they might be involved in its preparation, perhaps by collecting evidence or writing policies, or they might use it to make a judgement on a development proposal. Equally, a planner in the private sector might be interpreting the contents and direction of a plan for the benefit of their client. As a noun, the term 'plan' is defined by Oxford Dictionaries as a 'detailed proposal for doing or achieving something' and 'a diagram showing how something will be arranged'. As a verb, the word 'plan' is defined as something to 'decide on and make arrangements for in advance'. A space-based plan contains both elements. It includes a written strategy and a series of proposals, as well as a visual plan that represents what is being envisaged.

Plans can be prepared at a range of spatial scales for a variety of locations across the built and natural environment. The length and complexity of these plans will vary, as well as the resources and time needed to prepare them. Some plans will arise from the community, while other plans will be imposed from above. Some plans will be fixed upon short-term goals, while others will be broader and look to the long term. Most plans will arise from planners working in the public sector, but some might also be prepared or supported by planners working in the private sector.

Plans and decision-making

The terminology used to describe plans varies with geography, as does the way in which plans are used to influence and direct development decisions on the ground. For the majority of the world, plans provide the foundation for a zonal system of planning. These plans, which are supported by legal ordinances, classify land use into a range of categories that then link to a range of parameters about what is or is not acceptable.

As the next chapter explains, this system provides considerable certainty to developers but it does require significant effort up front to zone and codify the land and to develop the ordinance. It also contrasts with the system in the UK, which is 'plan-led' but allows for an appropriate amount of discretion to enable an individual project to be considered on its own merits.

As the Planning Portal (2018) explains, a plan-led system is built on the principle 'that the decisions upon planning applications should be made in accordance with the adopted development plan, unless there are other material considerations that may indicate otherwise'.

The adopted development plan therefore has weight in legislative terms, leading it to be sometimes called the 'statutory plan'. You will read more about the associated material considerations in the next chapter, but broadly speaking, these considerations must:

- relate to the purpose of planning legislation, which is to regulate the development and use of land in the public interest;
- fairly and reasonably relate to the application concerned.

Example considerations include consultation responses from statutory and non-statutory bodies, the planning history of the site, national policy, and the design and character of the surrounding area.

The plan-led system is actioned in legislative terms in England and Wales by section 38(6) of the Planning and Compulsory Purchase Act 2004, in Northern Ireland by section 6(4) of the Planning Act (Northern Ireland) 2011, and in Scotland by section 25 of the Planning etc Act 2006. As explained below, the form of the development plan has changed and does not necessarily entail a single document.

Practising the plan-led system in the UK: Local Plans

The adopted development plan comprises either a Local Plan (England) or a Local Development Plan (rest of the UK), which local planning authorities are expected to produce. In some cases, the statutory development plan might also include an overarching strategic plan (England and Scotland) or neighbourhood plan (England). The form and process by which the plans are produced are shaped by national policy. Legislation, circulars and letters from Chief Planning Officers provide further definition. English plans need to follow the policy prompts of the *National Planning Policy Framework* (NPPF), which outlines policy expectations over sixty or so pages. The framework was first published in 2012 (DCLG, 2012) and replaced a broader and more expansive suite of policy. A 2018 update has recently been published (MHCLG, 2018). The framework is supplemented by an online resource, *Planning Practice Guidance*, that expands guidance in certain areas and offers prescription to those producing plans.[1] Elsewhere, local planning authorities in Wales need to have regard to *Planning Policy Wales* and a series of Technical Advice Notes (Welsh Government, 2008, 2016), while planners in Scotland need to refer to *Scottish Planning Policy* and a number of Planning Advice Notes (Scottish Government, 2014a, 2014b). Similarly, planners in Northern Ireland need to refer to a suite of Planning Policy Statements (Department for Infrastructure, 2012, 2015).

Alongside these documents, planners in Wales, Scotland and Northern Ireland are also expected to refer to some overarching spatial frameworks that seek to give a spatial dimension to national policy. These documents include the *Wales Spatial Plan* (and a revised National Development Framework currently being prepared), the *National Planning Framework 3* in Scotland and the *Regional Development Strategy 2035* and the *Strategic Planning Policy Statement* in Northern Ireland (Welsh Government, 2008; Department for Infrastructure, 2012, 2015; and Scottish Government, 2014, respectively). England does not have an equivalent document but spatial priorities are presented through a myriad of publications.

Irrespective of their location, Local Plans are expected to be aspirational but realistic. They should present policies and proposals on what will, or will not, be permitted, and present a coordinated strategy for responding to economic, social and environmental challenges.

Although Local Plans vary, it is typical for them to include:

- a spatial description of the area being planned, with details of its geography and history, and its perceived strengths and challenges – such a survey normally follows a review of relevant evidence and is informed by public and stakeholder feedback;
- a vision, supported by strategic objectives;
- policies and proposals, to help deliver the vision;
- a strategy to help implement the plan and a framework for monitoring and review;
- a diagram or a visual representation of the plan.

Spatial description

Before preparing a plan or a policy it is important to understand the challenges and requirements of the area. The best way of achieving this is to undertake a physical survey of the space being planned. Patrick Geddes (1854–1932), a Scottish biologist, sociologist, geographer and town planner, famously coined the phrase 'diagnosis before treatment', and encouraged those creating civic plans to understand the geology, geography, climate, economic activity and so-called 'social institutions of the city'.

Walking around the area being planned will certainly prove a useful experience and will help to highlight such issues as road congestion, changing land use, derelict buildings and vacant land. A physical survey is also important to identify the significance of topography and key views, the safety and attractiveness of open space, or the physical condition of historic buildings. Observations gained in the field will be supplemented with other forms of data that will arise from desk-based research or some form of survey, such as the census that is actioned each decade across the UK. All of this material forms the plan's evidence base. While there are certain limits as to what can be collected, given time and cost constraints, the depth of a plan's supporting evidence is often used to determine the robustness and 'soundness' of a plan and its policies. A rich body of up-to-date evidence can help to:

- define the kind of problems that need resolving;
- inform the plan's overall vision and help to set up individual objectives;
- develop potential solutions;
- identify key groups and organisations who can offer help in supporting the plan's delivery;
- establish targets to help monitor the implementation of the plan.

Evidence will typically be needed for every theme or topic covered by the plan. This therefore means that information is likely to be required on the following:

- demographic structure;
- composition of the housing stock;
- size and composition of households;

- level of housing demand, by cost and type;
- levels of employability and occupation by sector;
- accessibility and levels of car use;
- levels of personal health, including rates of obesity;
- levels of local income and rates of deprivation;
- adequacy and accessibility of services and facilities;
- data relating to the historic environment, such as the positioning of conservation areas and listed buildings;
- data relating to the natural environment, such as the location of important ecological sites;
- environmental data, such as air quality, ground conditions and areas of flood risk;
- educational achievement;
- levels of crime and perceptions over personal safety;
- the form and reliability of transport infrastructure.

Vision

Each plan will be different and will vary with the geography and challenges of the area being planned. A typical starting point, by collecting and analysing the type of evidence discussed above, is to develop an overarching vision for the plan that can articulate the type of place being sought. The vision, which should help to anticipate and create a future, should be grounded by the local context and offer thoughts about where development should take place and where it should not. A plan's vision is typically expressed via a short block of text such as the partial example here that is included in a recently adopted (November 2017) joint plan for three settlements in Gloucestershire (Gloucester, Cheltenham and Tewkesbury):

> By 2031 Gloucester City, Cheltenham Borough and Tewkesbury Borough will have continued to develop as highly attractive and accessible places in which to live, work and socialise. The Joint Core Strategy area will be recognised nationally as enjoying a vibrant, competitive economy with increased job opportunities and a strong reputation for being an attractive place in which

to invest. The character and identity of individual communities will have been retained while improved access to housing will have addressed the needs of young families, single people and the elderly. New developments will have been built to the highest possible standards of design and focused on protecting the quality and distinctiveness of each community. (JCS, 2017: 11)

Strategic objectives

From the vision, a set of strategic objectives will normally follow (typically, between 10 and 20 objectives), and these will be focused upon some of the critical issues that have been identified. Collectively, they play a role in supporting the delivery of the spatial vision. Each objective needs to be clear, realistic and locally distinctive. The joint plan for Gloucester, Cheltenham and Tewkesbury has nine objectives, with these emphasising the need for:

- building a strong and competitive urban economy;
- ensuring the vitality of town centres;
- supporting a prosperous rural economy;
- conserving and enhancing the environment;
- delivering excellent design in new developments;
- meeting the challenges of climate change;
- promoting sustainable transport;
- delivering a wide choice of quality homes;
- promoting healthy communities.

Policies and proposals

The Cambridge Online Dictionary defines a policy as a set of 'ideas or a plan of what to do in particular situations'. Conversely, a proposal is defined as a 'suggestion' of how to achieve something. While a plan will have a mix of these, their number will vary depending on the context and focus of the plan. However, as a collective, they should set out the opportunities for development and help to satisfy the *strategic priorities* for the area. In England, the NPPF (MHCLG, 2018: 79) defines these as being:

- the homes and jobs needed in the area;
- the provision of retail, leisure and other commercial development;
- the provision of infrastructure for transport, telecommunications, waste management, water supply, wastewater, flood risk and coastal change management, and the provision of minerals and energy (including heat);
- the provision of health, security, community and cultural infrastructure and other local facilities;
- climate change mitigation and adaptation, conservation and enhancement of the natural and historic environment, including landscape.

A Local Plan will be expected to outline the level of housing and employment development felt to be necessary and will identify sites where this growth can be directed over a 10–15-year period. In doing so, it will be necessary for plan makers to have regard to relevant market and economic signals. While a plan will typically identify, by name, the largest and most strategic of opportunities, it will also acknowledge the role for smaller sites as land and buildings come forward (these are often known as windfall opportunities). Where appropriate, the plan will provide detail on the form, scale, and quantum of development, as well as detail on access and expected infrastructure investments. A Local Plan will also need to identify, and suitably justify, those areas where development would be inappropriate, for instance, in areas liable to flood risk or those that have environmental or historic significance. In addition to focusing on new forms of growth, a Local Plan will also present strategies for enhancing existing areas. These areas might form part of the natural or historic environment, or part of the urban area that requires regeneration. Equally, the plan might involve developing policy for ensuring access to housing, perhaps in a rural area.

These intentions will need to be actioned through a Local Plan's policies, which will be coded and listed numerically throughout the document. Policies tend to be presented via a bold font or included in a text box. Surrounding text on the page will help to justify or further explain the details of the policy. Some policies will simply outline the scale of growth needed, and the strategy for how the plan sees them being developed. Other policies will be restrictive in their nature, either by placing a universal constraint on development (with only limited exceptions) or setting criteria that identify the type of development and/or undertakings that would allow the development to be supported. Some policies can be lengthy while others can be short.

The Joint Core Strategy for Gloucester, Cheltenham and Tewkesbury (2011–2031) includes 32 policies, with the bulk of these targeting strategy and infrastructure provision, as shown in Table 5.1 (JCS, 2017).

Table 5.1: Strategy and infrastructure-based policies of the Gloucester, Cheltenham and Tewkesbury Joint Core Strategy

Strategic policies	The need for new development
	Distribution of new development
Strategy policies	Employment (except retail development)
	Retail and city/town centres
	Sustainable design and construction
	Design requirements
	Green belt
	Landscape
	The Cotswolds Area of Outstanding Natural Beauty
	Historic environment
	Biodiversity and geodiversity
	Residential development
	Housing mix and standards
	Affordable housing
	Gypsies, travellers and travelling show people
	Health and environmental quality
Infrastructure policies	Transport network
	Flood risk management
	Green infrastructure
	Social and community infrastructure
	Renewable energy/low-carbon energy development
	Infrastructure delivery
	Developer contributions

Although these policies are appropriate given the strategic nature of this joint plan, other local plans are more detailed and will provide policy on a far greater number of themes.

Visual material

Visual material will vary, but a plan will typically be accompanied by a strategic diagram that will indicate the broad position of strategic development and show the type of priority and policy being pursued across the area being planned. A proposals map will also accompany the plan and this will be issued on a scalable, map-based plan. A proposals map will normally show the following:

- planning and landscape designations, such as green belt or Areas of Outstanding Natural Beauty;
- sites allocated for development
- new road and transport proposals (including the safeguarding of certain routes for future investment);
- settlement boundaries;
- primary and secondary shopping areas;
- areas or corridors of open space;
- habitats and ecological and/or geological sites of international, national and local importance;
- areas of flood plain;
- conservation areas;
- historic parks and gardens;
- scheduled ancient monuments.

Some of the designations above will have a degree of familiarity to them but England's Planning Portal provides a helpful glossary via its website.[2]

The value of having a plan

Having a plan in place that outlines what an area's future intentions are, and what will happen where and when, provides certainty for communities, developers and infrastructure providers. Knowing about these intentions will also help to coordinate and maximise investment and ensure new development is complementary. For example, if major new housing development is to be directed to the south of a town, there might a stronger case for delivering a new hospital there compared to another location to the north of the town where the potential for additional housing development is far less. Equally, knowing about future development plans will also prove useful to transport providers and to the emergency services, who can seek to adapt their coverage accordingly. An area that has clarity, and a certain boldness, over its future is also likely to be in a stronger position for accessing funding and attracting investment. Critically, in terms of the UK at least, a clearly defined plan will allow a planning team to refuse or restrict development or certain activity from taking place in areas judged inappropriate or unsuitable. For example, a plan that allocates tranches of land in areas free of constraint will make it very hard for developers to make a case for development where the opposite is true.

Supplementary planning documents

As a supplement to the statutory plans outlined above, the planning systems of the UK also provide the opportunity for planning authorities to prepare Supplementary Planning Guidance (SPG) (Wales and Northern Ireland), Supplementary Guidance (SG) (Scotland), and Supplementary Planning Documents (SPD) (England). Despite the differences in name, this supplementary material can essentially provide further detail on the policies and proposals that are included in a statutory plan. As the NPPF explains, this type of guidance can also help applicants make better planning applications or assist with infrastructure delivery (MHCLG, 2018: 72). Supplementary guidance can be site-specific, for instance, in the form of a master plan for a site, or something that is more thematic. For example, Newport City Council in South Wales offers SPG on:

- affordable housing;
- archaeology;
- wildlife and development;
- house extensions and domestic outbuildings;
- new dwellings;
- flat conversions;
- parking standards.

In Scotland, some forms of SG can be treated as part of the statutory plan if certain procedures are followed.

Strategic plans

For certain matters it is acknowledged that plans need to extend beyond political boundaries which, in some cases, can be quite narrow. For example, a 'larger than local perspective' is likely to be necessary for certain forms of development, such as linear forms of infrastructure like rail lines that are more likely to be subject to topography and physical constraints than tightly defined political boundaries. Equally, a joined-up approach is necessary to ensure that the housing and employment needs of an area are directed to the right place in order for sustainability objectives to be met, which might not necessarily be in the same political area as that in which the demands have arisen. Strategic plans tend to be more conceptual and longer-term in their focus, and will avoid matters of detail and prescription. Consequently, while strategic plans tend to identify the scale of growth necessary, and the broad areas where it should be directed, they will avoid identifying every site that is likely to contribute. Rather than using a very detailed map base, diagrams included in a strategic plan tend to be more abstract and are characterised by symbols, arrows and areas of shading.

This strategic thinking can be captured in a variety of ways. Sometimes, it can be channelled into a separate plan or included at the start of a plan that focuses on more local matters thereafter. The geographical scale of a strategic plan can vary, from a document that looks at land and resources immediately surrounding the main urban area, to one that considers the broader city or sub-region. The status of these plans, in terms of whether they impact on projects on the ground, also varies.

England is a good example for both of these variables. For example, from the late 1960s, county councils were required to produce structure plans that set strategy for different councils within a single county area (such as Berkshire or Hampshire). These structure plans formed part of the 'statutory development plan' and therefore had a specific role in shaping and directing local development decisions. These structure plans were then replaced by statutory regional plans from 2004 onwards. These regional plans, for areas such as southwest and southeast England, essentially brought together counties and individual planning authorities. These regional plans were short-lived, though, and by 2010, steps were being taken to remove the plans and to dissolve the regional mechanisms that had been established to create them.

While planning in England today no longer has any formal (or statutory) regional or county plans, local councils are expected to work together under a mechanism called the 'duty to cooperate'. Other councils have also opted to create joint plans that allow for their respective council areas to be planned as a single unit. Some of this joint planning takes place voluntarily, while other authorities have formally joined their planning operations via so-called 'combined authorities'. Strategic influence in England is also provided via a series of Local Economic Partnerships and Local Nature Partnerships, which bring together relevant stakeholders connected with business development and environmental enhancement.

Strategic planning does have greater currency elsewhere, including other areas of the UK. For instance, SDPs are still prepared for certain areas of Scotland.

Neighbourhood plans

Although local communities provide important support to the preparation of authority-wide local plans, communities can, and have, prepared their own visions for how they see their settlement evolving. Examples include so-called community or parish plans. These documents can either be used as a source of evidence to shape broader plan-making activities, or be converted into standalone plans that developers can consult. In the past, these community plans have not had any formal status with respect to decision-making. However, in England the Localism Act 2011 allows for neighbourhood forums and parish councils to create neighbourhood plans. Forums and councils are required to identify an area which they want to plan for. The relevant local planning authority must agree to this before work on the neighbourhood plan can begin. Neighbourhood plans need to respond to the strategic context provided by the Local Plan, have regard to national planning policy, and be compatible with EU obligations and human rights requirements.

Once a neighbourhood plan has been prepared, its support needs to be measured via a local referendum. If the plan is supported, and has been found to be sound via a public examination, it becomes part of the adopted (statutory) development plan. Planning decisions for the area must then be taken in accordance with the neighbourhood plan, as well as the relevant Local Plan for the wider area. Although the other parts of the UK are monitoring the rollout of neighbourhood plans, there have been no allowances, as yet, to incorporate these community-driven plans into the adopted development plans of the other nations.

Table 5.2 offers a summary of how the plan-led system is operationalised across the UK.

Table 5.2: Operation of the plan-led system across the UK

	National policy	Composition of the statutory development plan	Number of local planning authorities
England	National Planning Policy Framework (NPPF) (2018) National Planning Policy Guidance (NPPG) – an online resource that extends the policy direction of the NPPF	Local Plan – as produced by a local planning authority Neighbourhood Plan – where one has been produced Waste and Mineral Plans – as produced by county council planning teams	27 County Councils (upper tier) 201 district councils (lower tier) 36 metropolitan boroughs (unitary) 32 London boroughs (unitary) 55 unitary authorities (unitary) 2 *sui generis* authorities – City of London Corporation and Isles of Scilly (unitary)

continued ...

	National policy	Composition of the statutory development plan	Number of local planning authorities
Northern Ireland	Regional Development Strategy 2035 (2012) – presents overarching strategic guidance Strategic Planning Policy Statement for Northern Ireland (2015) – presents regional planning policies for securing orderly and consistent development across Northern Ireland (2015) Planning Policy Statements (various topics and publication dates)	Local Development Plan – as produced by each council area	11 councils
Scotland	National Planning Framework 3 (2014) – adds a spatial dimension to Scotland's economic and investment plans Scottish Planning Policy (2014) – outlines the policy context for a range of planning themes Planning Advice Notes (various) – provide advice on good practice	Strategic Development Plan (SDP) – required to be prepared for the four largest city regions (Aberdeen, Dundee, Edinburgh and Glasgow) Local Development Plan (LDP) – as produced by a local planning authority Supplementary Guidance – where certain legal requirements have been met	32 unitary authorities plus two National Park authorities

continued ...

	National policy	Composition of the statutory development plan	Number of local planning authorities
Wales	Planning Policy Wales (Edition 9, 2016) – presents land use policy for Wales. Although previously contained in a separate document, this publication also includes policy on minerals and waste Wales Spatial Plan (2004, updated in 2008) – sets strategic planning priorities for Wales (will be replaced by a National Development Framework that is currently under production) Technical Advice Notes (various) – expand on the policy presented in Planning Policy Wales	Local Development Plan – as produced by a local planning authority	22 unitary authorities

Plan-making processes

The process for creating a plan will vary by geography and its intended purpose, while policy and legislation is likely to determine timescales and specific undertakings. Figure 5.1 provides an overview of the basic steps involved in producing a Local Plan in England. Of course, this is a basic representation and there is more interactivity between the stages shown. While the diagram shows a linear process, in reality it is cyclical, as evidence arising from the monitoring and review stage will help to inform a future review of the plan.

Figure 5.1: Stages in the production of a Local Plan

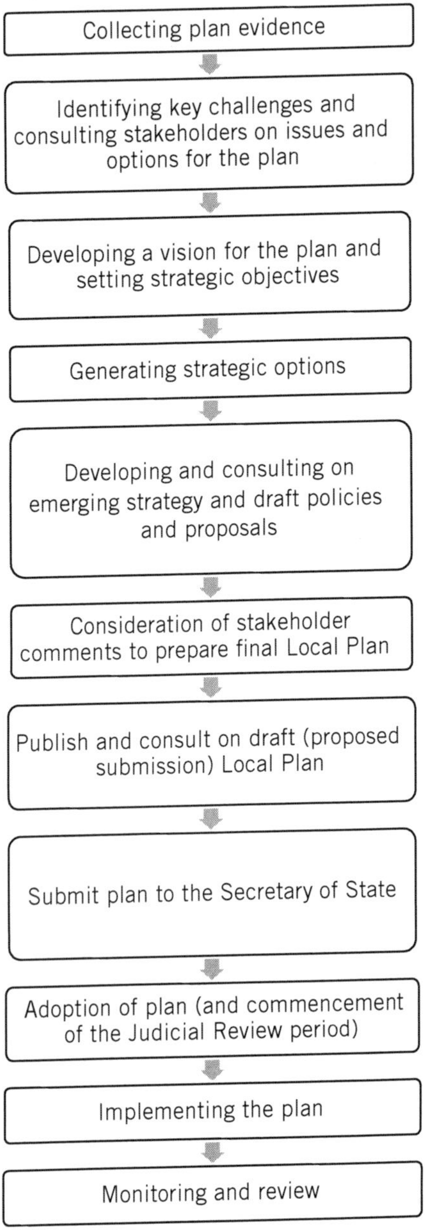

Collecting plan evidence

↓

Identifying key challenges and consulting stakeholders on issues and options for the plan

↓

Developing a vision for the plan and setting strategic objectives

↓

Generating strategic options

↓

Developing and consulting on emerging strategy and draft policies and proposals

↓

Consideration of stakeholder comments to prepare final Local Plan

↓

Publish and consult on draft (proposed submission) Local Plan

↓

Submit plan to the Secretary of State

↓

Adoption of plan (and commencement of the Judicial Review period)

↓

Implementing the plan

↓

Monitoring and review

Creating a plan takes time and appropriate allowances must be made to ensure that the expectations and requirements of each stage are adhered to. Table 5.3 shows the timeframe for reviewing the Local Plan of Camden, London. The plan covers the period 2016–31 and replaces a previous version published in 2010.

Table 5.3: Stages in the production of the Camden Local Plan

Initial engagement on issues and options	Late 2013
Consultation on a pre-submission and draft Local Plan	Early 2015
Consultation on a submission version of the Camden Local Plan	February to April 2016
Plan submitted for examination	June 2016
Examination of plan	October 2016
Consultation on plan modifications arising from the examination	January to March 2017
Publication of the Examiner's Report	May 2017
Adoption of the Camden Local Plan	July 2017

Plan making and community involvement

The Royal Town Planning Institute (RTPI) explains how community involvement is designed to create 'effective interactions between planners, decision-makers, individual and representative stakeholders to identify issues and exchange views on a continuous basis' (RTPI, 2005: 4). While much of the focus is typically directed to those residents who live in the area being planned, plan makers also need to engage with anyone who has an interest in the area. This could be because they work in the area, own property or land, operate infrastructure, or have a role in managing land or resources. Collectively, these people or groups, from either the public, voluntary or private sectors, are typically described as stakeholders.

Whatever the focus of the group or individual, securing their engagement can offer a multitude of benefits, such as:

- **Helping to limit opposition to development projects.** By involving the public and other key stakeholders, it is hoped that project drivers and design decisions can be understood and appreciated.
- **Making plans and projects better.** While involvement can often generate concerns that increased public involvement will lead to increased public opposition, it can also help to generate ideas or interventions for improving the project. Involvement might also allow for local intelligence about the site to be shared with the development team, such as information about former site activity or observations concerning site constraints.
- **Helping to build interest in the plan or project.** Involvement allows for information about the scheme to be shared early on and could offer elements of promotion that could ultimately lead to greater uptake and use of the scheme being developed.
- **Contributing to improved knowledge about planning, development and the needs of businesses and communities.** Involvement can also help to improve knowledge about how government works and support wider initiatives for encouraging a vibrant, open and participatory democracy.

Despite these benefits, involvement can often generate concerns surrounding cost and the delays that effective involvement can bring to project delivery. There are also concerns over whether involvement can attract undue negativity, or whether engagement activity will help to air the views of the few rather than the many. While there is validity to some of these points, negative impacts can be limited through effective planning and management.

As Wates (2014) explains, a range of tools exist for securing involvement. The website communityplanning.net lists over forty, but the following three are the most common:

- **public exhibitions or meetings**, where details about a project or plan are shared via information boards or a presentation and can be discussed with attending project staff;

- **project website**, where details of a plan or project can be read and commented on online;
- **design workshop**, where the public and other key stakeholders can contribute to more detailed exercises or discussions about a plan or project.

The appropriateness of different tools will vary with each plan or project, but it is likely that a combination of different methods will be necessary. Whatever the approach, steps to encourage involvement need to be visible so that people are aware of the opportunities available to them. Methods also need to be accessible and inclusive to attract the broadest range of participants, with regard being given to accessing so-called 'hard-to-reach' groups. Such a term is a little fuzzy, and will depend on local context, but often includes young people and young families.

Reaching out to disabled, racial, ethnic, linguistic or religious minority groups may require certain action to be taken, but the involvement of as many parties as possible, and consideration of their views, will be beneficial to the planning project being progressed.

As RTPI (2005) guidance explains, engagement should be timely and conducted at a time when changes to the scheme or plan can still be made. If the public feel that they are being consulted on matters that have already been decided then they are unlikely to get involved. Linked to this, and to avoid so-called consultation fatigue, broader engagement by a developer or a planning authority should be carefully coordinated. Similarly, in undertaking the engagement, the RTPI (2005) explains how it is necessary for staff to be suitably transparent and to disclose relevant details about the plan or project. Holding details back will do very little to establish trust between the engaging parties.

Successful engagement also requires an element of 'feeding back' in order to present an accurate picture of the comments received and a summary of how the scheme or plan has been changed in response (and appropriate explanations where no action has been taken). Such a process is often enhanced where sensible expectations are set at the start of the involvement. While an end goal should be to establish 'win-win' solutions, it is probably unrealistic to expect all issues be designed out.

In Scotland, plan-making teams must include a Participation Statement that explains how, and with whom, involvement in preparing the local plan will be managed.

Sustainability appraisal

In addition to responding to public and stakeholder feedback, and to the direction offered by national policy, planners will also need to ensure that the policies and proposals of their plan are compatible. Assessing the fit of the plan with previously set goals will also be important. These will vary, but the pursuit of greater sustainability will be a core goal, with the UN's 17 goals for sustainable development being a key reference point. This is certainly the case in England, with the NPPF requiring that Local Plans be prepared with the objective of contributing to the achievement of sustainable development (United Nations, 2015).

Assessing plan content via a kind of sustainability matrix is common, with the UK having an established reputation within the field. In England, local and neighbourhood plans are required to be assessed via a Sustainability Appraisal (SA), which needs to progress systematically through the plan-making process. The SA's overall goal is to promote sustainable development and to assess the fit of policies and proposals around this goal. The process starts with the accumulation of a baseline of evidence that can describe the characteristics of the area and the sustainability challenges that need to be addressed. The public and other key stakeholders are involved in shaping this baseline, which is then used to assess the appropriateness of the plan's vision and associated objectives and, in time, the policies and proposals of the plan. As each stage of the plan-making progresses, the SA is expected to inform the thinking being advanced and to help identify potential alternatives where any kind of negative impact is anticipated.

For those policies and proposals where a negative impact seems inevitable, the SA is used to identify the kind of mitigation that can be applied to help provide some resolution and potentially transform the impact from being negative to positive: Although SAs can be long and voluminous, they do not need to be and can provide invaluable intelligence on the decisions that have been made in creating the plan. The approach to SA in England, as well as the broader UK, incorporates the requirements of the Environmental Assessment of Plans and Programmes Regulations 2004, which in turn incorporates the requirements of the EU's Strategic Environmental Assessment (SEA) Directive (Directive 2001/42/EC). Although the SEA Directive interprets the 'environment' in broad terms, SA does have a broader pitch and will give appropriate attention to social and economic objectives as well. Alongside an SA, other plans may be subject to other kinds of assessment, such as that required by the Habitat Regulations Assessment, which implements legislation surrounding the protection of European habitats and species.

Project management

Keeping track of plan-making activity can be difficult, but it is important for the public and other key stakeholders to engage and respond where necessary. Responses will be predicated for a range of reasons. Developers will want to promote their sites, while residents may be wanting to ensure proposals satisfy any concerns they might have. To help keep groups and individuals informed, it is typical for plan-making teams to prepare a timeline and schedule to detail the plans being produced and the dates when consultation is expected. Indeed, in England, local planning authorities are required to communicate this information via a Local Development Scheme, which needs to be kept up to date and made available on the council's website.

Examination

Plan-making activity typically concludes with some kind of examination or independent review. The former occurs in England and requires the local planning authority to send a copy of their Local

Plan (submission version), together with any suggested changes and supporting documents (such as the SA), to the Planning Inspectorate. The Planning Inspectorate, acting on behalf of the Secretary of State, appoints an Inspector to examine whether the Local Plan has been prepared in line with the relevant legal requirements (for example, duty to cooperate) and whether the plan meets a list of so-called 'tests of soundness'. These tests seek to ensure that the plan has been:

- **positively prepared** – the plan pursues a strategy that seeks to meet objectively assessed development and infrastructure requirements;
- **justified** – the plan should be considered the most appropriate strategy, when considered against the reasonable alternatives, based on proportionate evidence;
- **effective** – the plan should be deliverable over its period and apply effective joint working on cross-boundary strategic priorities;
- **consistent with national policy** – the plan should enable the delivery of sustainable development in accordance with the policies of the NPPF (DCLG, 2012: para 182).

During the examination, the Local Planning Authority can ask the Inspector to recommend modifications that would make the plan sound or allow it to have greater compliance with legislation (this happened in the Camden example above). Following the examination, the Inspector will issue a report that will state whether the Local Plan can be adopted by the Local Planning Authority. If that is not the case then the plan-making team will need to return to an earlier stage and address the deficiency identified. Once a plan is adopted, there is a period of six weeks when external parties can seek a judicial review to try and stop the plan being implemented. Such a challenge needs to focus on procedural oversight and needs to be made within a set timeframe (6 weeks).

Delivery and implementation

Plan-making can be a lengthy process. While each plan is likely to be developed through similar stages, plans are created against a dynamic backdrop that can often impact on delivery and implementation. This type of change can arise in response to a range of factors, such as a shift in political power, changes in socio-economic trends or conditions, or a change in government policy. For the latter, a national change in the attitudes towards housing delivery, or a revised position concerning the strategic protection of land, can potentially have a significant impact upon a plan's status and its ability to meet its stated goals.

The resources that are available to create a plan can also be the subject of change, such as the significant cuts to public sector resourcing that have been applied as part of a UK-wide austerity programme. A shrinking team of planners, or a team devoid of certain skills or areas of knowledge, is unlikely to create a plan at the required pace or of the expected quality. This lack of resource has been cited as one of many factors that have led to low local plan coverage in England, with plans becoming outdated or being unable to satisfy set growth targets. Indeed, a recent study from the Ministry of Housing, Communities and Local Government (MHCLG) highlighted how over forty per cent of local planning authorities in England do not have a plan that meets the projected growth in households in their area (MHCLG, 2018).

Alongside more contextual factors, other commentators have helped to identify criteria for securing the 'perfect implementation' of policy. Dorey (2014) provides a particularly useful set, and these are outlined in the next chapter. Alongside these overarching factors, plan makers must ensure their plans are *feasible* and *viable*. Feasibility relates to the ability to adhere to or practise something conveniently or easily. It also has connotations with respect to probability in that a feasible scheme is one that is likely to happen. So, in a development sense, a feasible scheme would be one that accommodates an appropriate number of new homes commensurate to the size and form of the site, and access arrangements that can be delivered with the space and resources available.

Viability has a similar meaning, and the term 'financial viability' has significance to planners. Although a consideration of costs and values is often demanded at the project scale, particularly where discussions are under way about the level of financial contribution required for affordable housing or education, viability is also expected to be considered as and when plans, and their policies and proposals, are formed. Opinions about viability also need to be kept under review to safeguard against changing economic conditions. For planners to have an accurate picture of viability, views on value must be counterbalanced by a range of costs such as:

- **build costs**, reflecting the intended use;
- **abnormal costs**, such as those relating to the treatment of contaminated sites;
- **site-specific infrastructure costs**, such as access roads, drainage systems, green infrastructure or utility connections;
- **the cost of relevant policy requirements** that might require the applicant to make a financial contribution of some kind or to do something via their development that would generate a cost;
- **costs relating to finance**, such as those attached to financing loans;
- **professional fees**, relating to such services as planning, design, construction and surveying, project management, sales and marketing.

Monitoring and review

Given these potential issues over implementation, most plans will typically incorporate mechanisms through which the plan can be monitored and reviewed. For some plans there will be expectations that they will be reviewed after a certain period of time. For example, in England, there is an expectation that the statutory Local Plan is reviewed every five years. Monitoring documents typically refer to the following:

- a specific policy or proposal number with a summary of its general purpose or aim;
- a previously set indicator that the plan-making team felt would be appropriate for observing progress in satisfying the policy or proposal;
- a summary of the data and evidence being used to monitor progress;
- a view as to whether the policy or proposal is being actioned or progressed as intended;
- a proposed course of remedial action if the policy or proposal is not being delivered as intended or is leading to some unintended consequences.

Monitoring documents in an English context are known as Annual Monitoring Reports (AMRs). A particularly good example is the AMR produced by the Greater London Authority (GLA). The GLA, under its founding legislation, is required to produce such a document to measure the performance of the Mayor's London Plan. An AMR has been produced each year since 2005, with evaluative data being provided via the GLA's London Development Database (LDD), which brings together data on planning permissions and development completions from each of the London boroughs. Information is also provided by the GLA's Intelligence Unit and Environment Team, Transport for London, Historic England, the Environment Agency, and the Port of London (GLA, 2017).

Rather than assessing performance against an individual policy or proposal, the London AMR assesses performance against six underlying objectives that are embedded into the plan. For each objective the plan identifies a series of relevant key performance indicators (KPIs) that summarise the intended goals, together with some commentary over effectiveness. So, for objective five, which seeks to make London a world leader in improving the environment, eight specific KPIs are outlined:

- maximising at least 96% of new residential development on previously developed land;

- no net loss of open space designed for protection in local plans due to new development;
- no net loss of Sites of Importance for Nature Conservation;
- at least 45% of waste recycled/composted by 2015 and 0% of biodegradable or recyclable waste to landfill by 2026;
- annual average percentage of CO_2 emission savings for strategic development proposals progressing towards zero-carbon in residential development by 2016 and all developments by 2019;
- production of 8550 GWh of energy derived from renewable sources by 2026;
- increase in the total area of green roofs in the Central Activities Zone (CAZ);
- restore 15km of rivers and streams between 2009 and 2015, with an additional 10km by 2020 (GLA, 2017).

Conclusions

In this chapter we have explored and considered the role of plans, policies and proposals. We have considered the type of content that you will find in a plan and have identified some of the key steps that need to be taken when producing an aspirational, yet deliverable, plan. The next chapter focuses on the relationship between plans and the consideration of site development proposals.

Further reading

For a more detailed consideration of the matters discussed in this chapter, the following texts are recommended:

Couch, C. (2016) *Urban planning: An introduction*, Basingstoke: Palgrave.

Cullingworth, B., Nadin, V., Hart, T., Davoudi, S., Pendlebury, J., Vigar, G., Webb, D. and Townshend, T. (2015) *Town and country planning in the UK* (15th edn), Abingdon, Oxon: Routledge.

Hall, P. and Tewdwr-Jones, M. (2010) *Urban and regional planning*, London: Routledge.

Hopkins, L.D. (2007) *Engaging the future: Forecasts, scenarios, plans and projects*, Cambridge, MA: Lincoln Institute of Land Policy.

House of Commons Research (2016) *Comparison of the planning systems in the four UK countries*, London: House of Commons Library.

Planning Advisory Service (2014) *Good plan making guide*, London: PAS/Local Government Association.

Steiner, F. (2018) *Making plans: How to engage with landscape, design and the urban environment*, Austin, TX: University of Texas Press.

Websites

You can also find more detail about the systems around the UK, including details of the latest planning policy and legislation, via the websites below:

England (Ministry of Housing, Communities and Local Government): https://www.gov.uk/government/organisations/ministry-of-housing-communities-and-local-government

Northern Ireland (NI Direct): https://www.nidirect.gov.uk/articles/development-plans

Planning Portal: https://www.planningportal.co.uk

Scotland (Scottish Government: Building, Planning and Design): https://beta.gov.scot/building-planning-and-design/

Wales (Welsh Government: Planning): http://gov.wales/topics/planning/?lang=en

Current policy

While policy is subject to constant refresh, the following documents are current at the time of writing (October 2018):

Department for Infrastructure (2012) *Regional Development Strategy 2035*, Belfast: DfI Planning.

Department for Infrastructure (2015) *Strategic Planning Policy Statement*, Belfast: DfI Planning.

Ministry of Housing, Communities and Local Government (MHCLG) (2018) *National Planning Policy Framework*, London: MHCLG.

Scottish Government (2014) *National Planning Framework 3*, Edinburgh: Scottish Government.

Scottish Government (2014) *Scottish Planning Policy*, Edinburgh: Scottish Government.

Welsh Government (2008) *Wales Spatial Plan* (2nd edn), Cardiff: Welsh Government.

Welsh Government (2016) *Planning Policy Wales* (9th edn), Cardiff: Welsh Government.

Notes

1   https://www.gov.uk/government/collections/planning-practice-guidance
2   www.planningportal.co.uk

6

Planning in practice

Introduction

In this chapter we will explore how the planning system is operationalised to enable decision-making to take place. The planning decision-making space is sometimes placed under the umbrella of 'development management' because it is here that choices are actually made which will ultimate determine quite what is built and where; thus change is being managed. As the previous chapter explained, the UK has a relatively unique approach to planning decision-making, employing a 'discretionary' planning system. This creates a very particular and dynamic environment where decisions are made on a case-by-case basis. It is an interesting, flexible and 'live' context in which to work, which brings both challenges and opportunities.

The process of development

It is first important to appreciate the importance of terminology. In this chapter we will be using the word 'development' in two different ways:

1. Development to mean the process of undertaking change to land and/or a building; and
2. Development to mean the word upon which the legal scope of planning is defined.

Initially, before exploring the legal foundations of the system (the second way), we will consider the wider process of development (the first way) within which planning is functioning.

The process of development is essentially a way of looking at how change occurs; the steps that we can identify to help us understand what is actually happening within the process of change. The process of development is typically presented as the deconstructed steps through which we can understand the change that takes place in the built and natural environment; it is the steps involved in transitioning a building or piece of land from one use or condition to another. This can range from the reuse of a building, to demolition and rebuilding on a site, or the development of a new scheme on a site that was previously greenfield. Quite how the process of development is presented and is deconstructed depends upon the industry perspective concerned, but ultimately it consists of an interpretation of the steps taken between an idea coming forward until a property re-enters the process of development through disposal, redevelopment or reuse. In reality, it is very difficult to break these steps down into neatly compartmentalised stages, and during the process there will be overlap and some movement back and forth due to the demands and impacts of certain elements in the process. In academic and practice literature you will find that the process is presented slightly differently by authors who choose to break it down into differently titled, or a different number of, steps. This is understandable given that they will be talking to a target audience. For us, the model presented by John Ratcliffe, Michael Stubbs and Miles Keeping (2009) is a good one to work with because it is intended for students studying real estate, property and planning subjects. Drawing on their model as a guide, we can present the process of development as shown in Figure 6.1.

Figure 6.1: The process of development

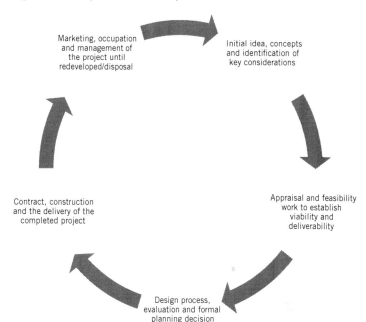

Marketing, occupation and management of the project until redeveloped/disposal

Initial idea, concepts and identification of key considerations

Contract, construction and the delivery of the completed project

Appraisal and feasibility work to establish viability and deliverability

Design process, evaluation and formal planning decision

Adapted from Ratcliffe et al (2009).

Each of the steps can be explained a little further as follows:

- **Initial idea, concepts and identification of key considerations:** This is the early stage when an idea is first being considered. At this point, the basic intentions are considered and the demands, requirements and challenges presented. Finances, site options, land ownership/rights and market demand/conditions are all examples of key considerations here.
- **Appraisal and feasibility work to establish viability and deliverability:** Having established a potential to progress the project, more detailed site surveys and investigations will be undertaken, initial discussions will be carried out with key decision makers, including the local planning authority, and

further work be done to ensure the finances are in place and a deliverable schedule developed.

- **Design process, evaluation and formal planning decision:** At this point the agreed scheme will be brought together and finalised by the team, with the architect playing a key role in many respects. With the scheme finalised, planning permission will be formally sought, alongside other necessary approvals such as Building Regulations.

- **Contract, construction and the delivery of the completed project:** With approval (hopefully) secured, delivery can now progress. To do this, contracts will be awarded and agreed and the actual construction undertaken. The contracts component is a good example of an element in the process of development that will not sit neatly in one step: in reality, contracts with some actors will have been agreed, at least in principle, in advance of this.

- **Marketing, occupation and management of the project until recycling/disposal:** Once the project nears completion, it can be marketed for occupation. This will take different forms depending upon whether the freehold will be sold, a tenant sought to rent or a freehold and leaseholder arrangement intended. With the building occupied, it must be manged by the responsible party. Ultimately, it will be reused, redeveloped and at some point disposed of, all as part of a new process cycle! (Adapted from Ratcliffe et al, 2009)

Planning as a system within the process of development

From the planning perspective, we can create our own cycle for the process of development where we are specifically considering matters which require formal Express Planning Permission. Planners, alongside a few other professionals such as architects, are relatively unique in interacting with the process of development from start to finish. Within each step there will be specific planning actions happening which support the wider activities and progress taking place. Planning professionals will have varying degrees and scope of engagement in the full process of development; for example, involvement in development finance will certainly vary between roles, but all will have some input and influence in most of the steps presented. It is also worth highlighting that 'planning' is not limited to the planning application; some aspects of planning occur outside of the application itself, including some legal and financial matters. Furthermore, many associated regimes, such as Advertisement Consent and Listed Building Consent, sit within the planning 'family'. For the purposes of this section of the chapter, we will focus specifically on the planning application process and related activities associated with Express Planning Permission.

The planning process can therefore be mapped in parallel to the overarching process of development as seen from the real estate/ property development perspective, with a set of five steps which sit alongside the five steps of the wider process, as shown in Figure 6.2.

Figure 6.2: The planning process of development

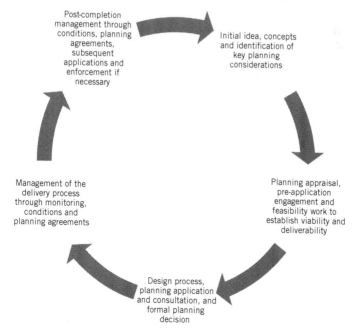

Post-completion management through conditions, planning agreements, subsequent applications and enforcement if necessary

Initial idea, concepts and identification of key planning considerations

Planning appraisal, pre-application engagement and feasibility work to establish viability and deliverability

Design process, planning application and consultation, and formal planning decision

Management of the delivery process through monitoring, conditions and planning agreements

Adapted from Ratcliffe et al (2009).

These steps can be explained a little further as follows:

- **Initial idea, concepts and identification of key planning considerations:** Planning is a key consideration at this early stage and private sector planning professionals in particular will be part of this step. The viability and deliverability of a project is heavily dependent upon whether the scheme will be able to successfully secure planning permission. Given this, exploring how the proposal responds to the policies in the Local Plan, Neighbourhood Plan (where there is one in place), national guidance and other policy/plan considerations will be a key element of the early research into a project. Other considerations around the likely site-specific implications will be part of this too: how will the local community react to the scheme, and what impact will it have on them? Can the site be successfully developed with regard to transport and movement matters? Design? Environmental impact? Landscape? Impact upon residential amenity? Can the scheme also deliver planning and/or investor requirements specific to the proposal – affordable housing, for example? And what impact does all this have on costs and financial viability? Planning, alongside key matters such as land ownership/rights and development finance, will be one of the most significant factors impacting on the initial consideration of feasibility associated with a new development idea.

- **Planning appraisal, pre-application engagement and feasibility work to establish viability and deliverability:** After an initial consideration of the planning 'potential' of a site, steps will now be taken to develop the ideas in collaboration/consultation with stakeholders, including communities, the local planning authority and key organisations appropriate to the site, for example, the Environment Agency, Historic England, Highways England and Natural England, or their equivalents in the other nations of the UK. During this stage the proposers of the development will seek to secure confidence that their scheme will achieve planning permission when the formal process is progressed. Pre-application discussions will vary in their degree of formality, and indeed cost, between local planning authorities, but the desired outcome is the same: maximum support for the development.

- **Design process, planning application and consultation, and formal planning decision:** Following revisions and the evolution of the design of the proposal as a result of the prior stage, the formal planning process will be engaged with. This will be discussed in more detail below, but essentially this is the very structured and formal phase of the planning process, where an application is submitted. This will be considered by the local planning authority, in consultation with stakeholders including the local community and expert advisors, and a formal decision will be made on the application.

- **Management of the delivery process through monitoring, conditions and planning agreements:** Having (hopefully!) secured planning permission, the development can progress in accordance with the agreed provisions. Planning conditions are attached to planning permissions to allow the implementation of the scheme to be managed effectively. Conditions can control how the development is undertaken (permitted days/hours of construction, for example); require further agreement of specific details (materials, landscaping, parking and cycle storage details, and so on); and provide long-term controls over the occupation, use and changes permitted for the scheme. In parallel, a planning agreement can be put in place. These are essentially legal agreements which allow for the impacts of planned change to be mitigated for and sustainable communities created. They can include the direct provision of, or monies to allow the provision of, affordable housing, green infrastructure (GI), wider highways and transport improvements, flood defence works, contributions to social and community infrastructure (schools, libraries and emergency services), and so forth. In combination, the planning decision, conditions and planning agreement enable effective change management in the built and natural environment.

- **Post-completion management through conditions, planning agreements, subsequent applications and**

enforcement if necessary: With the planning decision made, planning's influence does not end. Planning conditions can allow for control in perpetuity; subsequent changes to buildings brought about through redevelopment or expansion can require further permissions; and on some occasions, there will be a need for planning enforcement action to be taken. Planning really is an 'end-to-end' activity! (Adapted from Ratcliffe et al, 2009)

The building blocks of the system: 'development' and what this means

All systems of control need a scope/range of influence. Planning exists to do a specific job and is only one of a series of legislative regimes which exist to manage our built and natural environments. Each of these different systems of management therefore has a specific purpose, and they interlink to provide comprehensive controls, as illustrated in Figure 6.3.

Town and country planning therefore needs to define its scope and role, and have a basis of operation, sitting within the other interrelated management systems. Planning defines its scope in the first instance through one word: 'development'. Whether something is considered to be development or not determines whether something falls within the influence and scope of the planning system. Around the UK the definition of development is found in different pieces of national legislation, but it is ultimately the same: 'Development' is any building, mining, engineering or other operations which are carried out in, on, over or under land, or the making of a material change of use of buildings or other land (Sheppard et al, 2017).

One of the characteristics of UK planning can immediately be identified from the definition above: planning legislation relies upon the written word and this demands interpretation. It is also the case that in the UK a common law model is in place (hybrid in Scotland, where common law and civil law models can both be found). What this means for planning is that we must look both to legislation and to the courts for clarity in our understanding of quite what

Figure 6.3: The 'network' of legislation

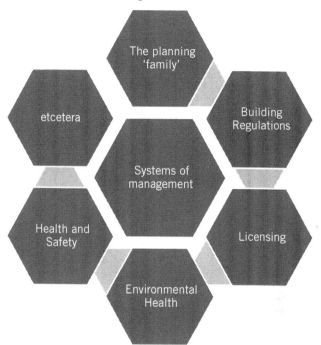

Adam Sheppard (2018).

this definition of development means. We can break this definition down into its component parts to help us with our understanding (Sheppard et al, 2017):

- **Building:** The most involved element of the definition, a building is any 'structure or erection'. This certainly goes beyond common understandings of what a 'building' is, since it can include 'structures'. Our interpretation of whether a structure or erection falls under the definition of a building is helped by case law, which has determined through a series of cases that it is the size, degree of permanency and physical attachment to the land that we use to make a judgement. This is an important point in itself: the decision is one of professional judgement and interpretation; there is no all-encompassing definition to rely upon. It is also not a 'tick-box' approach; a planner must weigh up the particular structure or erection and make a judgement for that specific instance and decide if it is indeed a building.

- **Mining and engineering:** These are very particular forms of development which we can understand through the common interpretation of the terms. Unlike 'building', which needs deconstructing, 'mining' and 'engineering' have adequate common interpretation which is accepted by planning. One important consideration to bring in here, though, is the question of scale. Planning operates on the principle of proportionality (which will be explored in greater detail below), which means that in the context of mining and engineering, some common sense is applied. A person digging with a spade, for example, wouldn't, from a planning perspective, be seen as undertaking an engineering operation in the vast majority of circumstances, but there will be a point where, as a result of the scale of operation or the equipment being used, the activities do become an engineering operation in the eyes of planning.

- **Other operations:** This is a bit of a 'catch-all' for planning. It essentially allows for things that don't fit into the rest of the definition but are important matters to be brought within the control of planning. Examples of this would be external shutters on shopfronts or some permanent and substantial awnings.

- **The making of a material change of use:** This aspect of the definition can be seen as a separate (but related) part of what constitutes development. There is the 'operational' or physical half of the definition – building, mining, engineering and other operations – and the 'material change of use' half. This is the bit that controls how land and buildings are used, and how this can change. Development occurs when there is a material change to the way in which the land or building is used. To be 'material', a change must essentially mean that something changes 'use class'. Use classes are the way in which planning essentially organises and manages uses. Planning categorises comparable uses, with similar impacts, into 'classes'. Changing from one use to another within the same class category is not development; changing use between classes is development. How these uses are broken down into classes varies between the nations of the UK, but the principle and basic approach is universal. Table 6.1 gives a simplified arrangement showing how planning systems around the UK categorise uses to enable their management.

We can further our understanding of 'development' by looking at what we specifically know *is not* development. This can be drawn from two sources: legislation and the courts. The courts have told us that very small alterations that do not materially impact the appearance of a property – an exterior light or alarm box, perhaps – may not be considered development but regarded as *de minimis* (too minor). In addition, 'ancillary' activities will not constitute development. These are essentially secondary activities taking place which are different in themselves, but related to, required for and dependent upon a primary use (for example, a staff canteen). Meanwhile, legislation tells us that the following are not development:

- internal works;
- use incidental to the enjoyment of a dwelling house – for example, carrying out hobbies or sometimes home working;
- statutory undertaker[1] activities – some road maintenance, for example;
- agricultural and forestry uses;
- change of use within the same class.

If we put the things that we know are not development together with our understanding of the definition of development, we can appreciate that planning has a very broad scope and influence over a significant proportion of the changes that can take place in our built and natural environment. All development requires planning permission one way or another; the important question is how that planning permission is then conferred.

Table 6.1: Planning use classes overview

England	Wales	Northern Ireland	Scotland
A1 Shops	A1 Shops	A1 Shops	Class 1 Shops
A2 Financial and professional services	A2 Financial and professional services	A2 Financial, professional and other services	Class 2 Financial, professional and other services
A3 Food and drink: restaurants and cafes	A3 Food and drink restaurants and cafes	B1 Business	Class 3 Food and drink
A4 Drinking establishments	B1 Business	B2 Light industrial	Class 4 Business
A5 Hot food takeaways	B2 General industry: industrial process other than that falling within B1	B3 General industrial	Class 5 General industrial
B1 Business	B8 Storage or distribution	B4 Storage or distribution	Class 6 Storage or distribution
B2 General industry: industrial process other than that falling within B1	C1 Hotels	C1 Dwelling houses	Class 7 Hotels and hostels
B8 Storage or distribution	C2 Residential institutions	C2 Guest houses	Class 8 Residential institutions
C1 Hotels	C3 Dwelling houses	C3 Residential institutions	Class 9 Houses
C2 Residential institutions	C4 Houses in multiple occupation	C4 Secure residential institutions	Class 10 Non-residential institutions
C2a Secure residential institutions	D1 Non-residential institutions	D1 Community and cultural	Class 11 Assembly and leisure
C3 Dwelling houses	D2 Assembly and leisure	D2 Assembly and leisure	
C4 Houses in multiple occupation			
D1 Non-residential institutions			
D2 Assembly and leisure			

Table from Sheppard et al (201

The proportionality principle

The rule underpinning the manner in which planning permission is conferred is the proportionality principle. It would be quite inappropriate and unmanageable if every single thing that needed planning permission required a planning application. As a result, there are different ways that planning permission can be secured. Each of these will be considered in the sections below, but they can be presented as shown in Figure 6.4.

This proportionality principle is underpinned by *impact*. Planning's intervention into our lives is legitimised through the necessity of balancing private wants with public interest. Therefore, where impact that merits government oversight occurs, planning has influence. In turn, where this impact exists, the *degree* of impact is significant: the greater the potential impact, the greater the legitimacy for state intervention into the decision and the more involved the manner of securing planning permission becomes.

As an aside, it is also possible to have planning permission conferred through deemed consent. This applies in some very particular cases where planning permission is not formally secured but is considered to be 'carried' by doing something else. The best example of this is probably Advertisement Consent (which is separate to planning permission). If we secure Advertisement Consent then planning permission is considered to exist as a result; it has deemed consent.

Figure 6.4: The proportionality principle

Developed from Sheppard et al (2017).

Permitted development rights

Permitted development rights are really important in ensuring that planning is proportionate and reasonable in its approach. Requiring a planning application for everything would be excessive and unjustifiable state intervention into our lives; it would also probably create an impossible work demand on local planning authorities. The planning system therefore provides permitted development rights, which are essentially allowances for small-scale developments which have planning permission conferred through a Development Order. The Development Order, published by the government, contains parameters for what has planning permission by being permitted development. If our development falls within these parameters, we can progress with the Development Order as the planning permission for our scheme. If we exceed the presented parameters, we will require approval from the local planning authority for our proposal (Sheppard et al, 2017).

Within the General Permitted Development Order there are lots of sections ('Parts') which give allowances for planning permission for different types of development, for example, house extensions, fences and walls, hardstanding (driveways and so on), alterations to non-residential buildings, and provisions for infrastructure-type works. Of note also are the allowances for changes of use. As we have seen, a change of use between use classes constitutes development; the General Permitted Development Order allows for some of these material changes to take place between use classes where this would have an acceptable impact. These allowances are underpinned by the proportionality principle: small-scale alterations that could not have (in the majority of circumstances) an impact of concern can proceed through permitted development rights. So, if we want to build a small extension, for example, this can often be done without a formal planning application (Sheppard et al, 2017).

One final point to mention concerning permitted development rights is that they are not universally applied. There are variations between each nation in the UK, but there is also more area-based variation. Within designated areas, such as national parks, conservation areas and Areas of Outstanding Natural Beauty, permitted development rights are more restricted. This is very understandable, because the areas are more sensitive and merit closer scrutiny and further protection. In addition, within local authorities it is possible to identify and approve areas for stricter or, indeed, more relaxed arrangements for permitted development rights through Article 4 Directions or Local Development Orders respectively. This is helpful because it means that where areas are more sensitive to change, they can be provided with additional protections of oversight, whereas in other situations where impacts of change might be less challenging (industrial estates, for example) greater flexibility can be offered. This allows the system to be reactive and to provide more or less flexibility as considered appropriate to the circumstances and sensitivity/opportunity in particular areas (Sheppard et al, 2017).

Prior approval

Sitting between permitted development and the need for a full planning application is prior approval. This is actually a form of permitted development but with an added requirement for local government approval over selected matters. The planning permission is therefore conferred by the General Permitted Development Order, but if it is a form of development that falls within certain parameters, an application for prior approval is required and approval must be secured from local government. In some respects, it is a middle ground where development is permitted but the potential for some specific problematic impact to occur justifies a limited degree of local government oversight throughout the prior approval process. Historically around the UK, prior approval arrangements were mainly associated with agricultural and telecommunications developments. So, for example, while small agricultural developments would be permitted development, some larger agricultural developments are permitted development but subject to prior approval from the local government concerning siting, design and external appearance. These are the only matters the local planning authority can consider in making their decision. Any development proposal that is more substantial needs a full application for planning permission (Sheppard et al, 2017).

This 'step' in the proportionality hierarchy does not exist for many types of development (so something is typically either permitted development or it needs a full planning application), but in England it has been used more frequently since the early 2010s, with agricultural buildings and office buildings securing new arrangements through prior approval for changes of use. These have proved controversial because they result in the local planning authority losing influence over development which may in certain circumstances actually be undesirable.

Planning applications and the pre-application phase

If a development falls outside the scope of the General Permitted Development Order then full planning permission is required. This is what we often associate with the idea of 'planning permission': the express act of sending a planning application to the local planning authority and seeking its approval.

In practice, before the planning application is made there is the pre-application phase. Looking back to the process of development (Figure 6.1) and the planning process of development (Figure 6.2), we can see that there is much to be done before we actually enter the formal planning system. Undertaking comprehensive research and analysis, including engagement with stakeholders such as the local community and key decision makers, is a really important part of ensuring that the best outcome can be achieved and a positive decision taken.

Having undertaken a (hopefully successful!) pre-application phase of work, a planning application can be submitted. Planning applications are formal submissions to secure planning permission from the local planning authority, and they must meet certain standards. A planning application will need to include all the required information appropriate to the type of development in question. This will involve submitting a form giving the details of the scheme, plans, a fee, and an ownership and agricultural holdings certificate, but also supporting statements covering key issues as necessary to allow the local planning authority to make an effective decision. A Design and Access Statement is a common requirement for larger-scale developments and more sensitive schemes, but additional materials addressing issues such as transport, environment, ecology, flooding, contamination, heritage, archaeology, retail impact and so forth may also be required to help the local planning authority to understand the scheme and make a decision (Sheppard et al, 2017).

Planning applications work through a specified process, with the submission initially checked for completeness, formally registered and allocated to a case officer, and the application advertised/consultations sent out so that everyone appropriate (the local community, key government agencies and so on) knows that it has been submitted. There follows a period of analysis, discussion and negotiation in response to the views of the case officer and other stakeholders before the decision is taken.

The decision itself will be a professional judgement; it will have regard to the development plan, and all other material considerations, and a balanced judgement will be taken. Private interest (the application proposal) is balanced against public interest (impact and implications for others), and the decision taken based on what is considered to be the 'best' outcome. Planning decisions are difficult because of the impossibility of planning – the inability to please everyone – but planning decisions will be evidence-based and taken using informed professional judgement, meaning the outcome should be as good as is possible (Sheppard et al, 2017).

Planning permission can actually be pursued in two ways through the standard planning system: one-stage or two-stage. The one-stage approach involves submitting a 'full' planning application. This will include all the details of the scheme and a single complete decision is made at the end of the process. The alternative is to take a two-stage approach by first securing outline planning permission, followed by reserved matters approval of details. An outline application essentially allows planning permission to be secured based on a more limited provision of detail (in line with a series of options that can be selected from), after which a reserved matters application can be submitted to deal with the details excluded from the outline scheme. The advantage of this two-stage approach is that it allows for the principle of development (the broad acceptability of the scheme) to be established, allowing certainty and confidence to be created before further money is spent pursuing the development. Outline planning permission can also be used to increase land values at the point of sale: a piece of land with planning permission for further development is worth more than an undeveloped piece of land.

Planning decisions

A planning decision is undertaken drawing on the principle of proportionality, while also enabling participation and democratic accountability in all cases. The 'power' to decide a planning decision is, following the established government principle of subsidiarity, given by central government to local government. Local government has typically established two key approaches to decision-making: committee decisions and 'delegated' decisions. In both cases the application goes through the same process of consultation, discussion, negotiation and evaluation, but how the ultimate decision is made varies. A delegated decision is one taken directly by the local planning authority's planning officers. This approach is applied for more minor applications which are not considered controversial by virtue of their scale, conformity with local planning policy, and level/ type of community and stakeholder consultation responses. Where applications are larger in scale, with greater impact potential, they are considered by a planning committee. This involves the planning officer presenting the application to the locally elected politicians ('Members'); hearing the views of the applicant, other stakeholders and the local community; and the Members then finally taking a vote on the planning application (Sheppard et al, 2017).

Planning decisions can sometimes be controversial because one 'side' or another will often be disappointed by a decision taken. This is understandable and unavoidable; the impossibility of planning is that it is impossible to manage change in the way that everyone wants because we all have different opinions and views on how places should evolve. What planning can do is try to ensure that the best decision is taken, in a democratic, transparent and accountable way, with effective engagement and participation, balancing private interests with public interests – no easy task!

Discretionary decisions

As noted in the previous chapters, a key characteristic of the planning system in the UK is that it is 'discretionary'. As you will have read, there are two basic types of planning system. The majority of planning systems are regulatory/zonal systems. These different names are applied to the same core approach: the 'plan' is essentially definitive and decisions are taken in line with the plan; it is a question of conformity. The planning application is effectively a broadly administrative process whereby a proposal is 'tested' against the plan in place: if the proposal is in line with the plan, it will be approved; if not, it will be refused. Plans will include different degrees of detail and there will be some variation in the process, but the core principles are based on this approach. In the UK, and in some other countries around the world, the system is different because it is discretionary; this means the plan remains extremely important, but it is not as binding as is the case in a regulatory/zonal system. This is the system that has developed over time but initially emerged in the UK through the Town and Country Planning Acts of 1947, and the system can best be described as a plan-led approach – the development plan (the 'adopted' local plan document) is the most important consideration in planning decisions, but 'other material considerations' can also be taken into account and, if these other material considerations merit it, a decision that is not necessarily in line with the plan can be taken. As the previous chapters noted, a material consideration can be almost anything that is deemed of significance to a planning decision, including national policy, supplementary policy, new emerging plans, new evidence in reports/ research and substantiated/valid views of stakeholders, for example (Sheppard et al, 2017).

In reality, looking at planning systems around the world, we find that they exist on a spectrum with different degrees of discretion (even if only through a court decision or plan change), or regulation/codification, existing. Systems do tend to broadly sit at one end or the other of the spectrum, though, with the UK system being probably the most discretionary approach that can be found. The debate over which approach is better is almost endless, but what we can briefly say is that there are certain key implications of each. A discretionary system is sometimes subject to criticism because it doesn't offer the absolute certainty that a plan does in a regulatory/codified/zonal system. This can be problematic for investors (who like certainty) and the development industry (which can find the lack of certainty frustrating). Contrary to this, however, a discretionary system creates a flexibility that makes the system dynamic and responsive, something all stakeholders (including developers, investors and applicants) can draw positives from.

Conditions

The story does not end when a decision is taken on a planning application. It is important for the planning system to continue to have influence over development so that it is built in line with the plan and constructed in an appropriate way, and so that final details of the scheme are approved and the future occupation/use and evolution of a building is acceptable. To facilitate this, planning conditions are used.

A planning condition is 'attached' to a planning decision and allows for controls in perpetuity. Conditions can control construction times; limitations on permitted development rights; and details concerning landscaping, materials, transport, environment, ecology, flooding, contamination, heritage, archaeology and so on; and may include management plans for matters such as public transport, open spaces, landscaping and such like. Conditions are important because they ensure that developments, once approved, remain acceptable in terms of their impact and do not evolve/change into something undesirable or harmful (Sheppard et al, 2017).

Planning gain

Alongside a planning application, we sometimes also find that planning gain is secured. Planning gain is not part of a planning application, but it is directly associated and tied to it. Planning gain essentially exists to permit the wider implications of development to be allowed for and mitigated or enhanced. The philosophy behind this is that when development takes place, it impacts upon the area, while, at the same time, profit is made. Planning gain is the capturing of some of this profit to mitigate the resulting impacts and ensure that society is properly provided for through physical and social infrastructure. A good example of this would be a new large-scale housing scheme: such a development would have an impact on traffic in the wider area, lead to requirements for new open spaces and parks, and place additional demands upon schools and other infrastructure. It could also create an opportunity for affordable housing to be provided and wider community benefits to be secured. Planning gain is the mechanism by which to do this. Planning gain is covered in more detail in Chapter 7.

Appeals and challenges

The planning decision taken is not necessarily final. As with most decisions taken by government, there is an ability to challenge it.

In planning systems around the world, challenges are typically available through the courts. This is essentially to test the legitimacy of a decision taken. In the UK, this is known as judicial review: an appeal made to the courts to test the legitimacy of the decision, that is, whether the decision was taken *correctly* in relation to process and procedure, and drawing on the appropriate evidence base.

Within the UK, alongside the opportunity for judicial review, another option also exists. This is a *merits-based* appeal. Such appeal types can only really exist in a discretionary planning system because what is being tested is not the *correctness* of the decision, but the *opinion* of the decision maker(s). As discussed previously, in a discretionary decision-making system, a decision is taken based on the plan and also other material consideration; this is a professional judgement. A merits-based appeal is essentially a way of securing a second, overriding, professional judgement on the accepted issues associated with the proposal. In the UK the merits-based appeal is pursued via a national-level organisation which is either a government agency (the Planning Inspectorate in England and Wales, or the Planning and Environmental Appeals Division of the Scottish Government) or, in Northern Ireland, an independent review body (the Planning Appeals Commission). Note that in Scotland it is only major development appeals which are managed directly by the national review body. More minor cases can be dealt with through local review bodies.

Differences exist in the details of the appeals approaches across the UK, but they all embrace the proportionality principle in their operationalisation. There are essentially three forms of appeal found, which, while having different names in the different systems of the UK, work on the same basis. These are shown in Figure 6.5.

Figure 6.5: Appeal formats

Adam Sheppard (2018).

In a little more detail, these steps can be explained as follows:

- **Written:** These appeals are essentially undertaken through an exchange of written documentation, sometimes just an appeal submission and a copy of the original case file. The inspector ('reporter' in Scotland, 'commissioner' in Northern Ireland) will review the case details and arguments presented by each party, visit the site, and issue a decision. In a planning appeal the decision will either be to dismiss the appeal and agree with the original decision of the local authority, or to 'uphold' the appeal and issue a new decision.

- **Informal:** Informal appeals, which may be called 'hearings', provide an opportunity for discussion. In addition to the written materials, which are still exchanged, and the site visit, an informal appeal brings in a roundtable discussion, led by the inspector/ reporter/commissioner. This creates an opportunity for the stakeholders to further express their views.

- **Formal:** This is the ultimate step in the hierarchy and replaces the informal roundtable discussion with a very formal interaction, which may be called an 'inquiry'. Again, there remains a written documentation exchange and a site visit, but the face-to-face discussion will have a far more formal character. Unlike a written or informal appeal process, a formal appeal scenario will feel more like a legal dispute resolution in some ways, including the case being managed and presented by lawyers rather than the planning team themselves. The stakeholders in the decision, including the planning officers, will present evidence under the direction of their legal team and will then be cross-examined by the legal team from the opposing side. It has parallels with a court appeal, with the inspector/reporter/commissioner acting almost as a 'judge', but it is normally held in less formal surroundings.

The different types of appeals have various advantages and disadvantages, but as a general point we can say that the further up the hierarchy we progress, the more expensive the process can become (appeals are themselves free, but everyone involved needs paying!) and the longer it can take, because it will be more involved. The advantage of taking steps up the hierarchy is that with each step there is an enhanced opportunity to really present and explore the case in detail; this is necessary for more complex and involved cases. As noted previously, this is the proportionality principle in action: the more complex and challenging the matter at hand, the great the need for legitimacy of the form of intervention. To ensure the planning and appeals systems are used appropriately and effectively, appeals allow for 'costs'. Costs are not tied to the decision; rather, they are about *behaviour* and whether the decision and the actors' behaviour in the planning decision and appeal were reasonable. This aims to ensure the effectiveness of both the appeals system and wider planning decision-making (Sheppard et al, 2017).

A final point about appeals relates to exactly who can appeal. In a court-based appeal (including UK judicial review) any 'interested party' can appeal. In a merits-based appeal in the UK, however, only the applicant and their representative can appeal. This excludes other interested parties and means that if, for example, an application is approved, other interested parties have no right to appeal this decision, whereas if it is refused, the applicant can decide to appeal this decision. For some, this is legitimately considered unfair and a failure to allow for a universal right to appeal, but others would argue that if the merits-based appeal system was opened to 'third parties', it would be abused by those wishing simply to prevent change (so-called NIMBYs) and the system would be overwhelmed.

System variations: nationally significant infrastructure and permission in principle

Brief mention is needed of other forms of planning decision-making. Around the UK, the majority of express planning decisions are made through the 'standard' application process discussed in this chapter. There are, however, circumstances where variation exists. A common example of this is 'calling in' applications. This is essentially where a decision, by virtue of its scale, implications or sensitivity, is not made by the local planning authority but taken instead by the respective national government within the UK. Beyond this, the most notable deviation is how nationally significant infrastructure is managed. In England, and to a lesser extent Wales (and occasionally Scotland), national infrastructure is dealt with directly by national government (via the Planning Inspectorate) through a bespoke and unique system. The basic approach to decision-making is to a certain extent comparable to a 'standard' planning application, with consultation and analysis/discussion/negotiation taking place, but the decision is taken in line with a specific set of national planning policy documents (developed with parliamentary approval), and at the end 'development consent' is (hopefully) secured (Sheppard et al, 2017).

The other approach meriting mention is permission in principle (PiP). This exists in England and is intended to bring more certainty into the system for housing developers. PiP is arguably an alternative to the two-stage approach of pursuing outline planning permission followed by reserved matters approval. PiP works in association with the Brownfield Land Register, which local authorities maintain. Land which is registered is taken into the Local Plan and designated within the plan as having PiP (this must be for residential, or residential-led mixed use, development). This land can then be developed by securing a 'technical consent' for the development of the land in question, which is akin to the reserved matters application stage. The advantage of this is that by being designated as having PiP in the Local Plan, developers have confidence that the land can be developed, in the same way that securing outline permission provides this reassurance, only the details need to be resolved. Critics might argue that land identified as having PiP would typically be land where outline planning permission could be secured, so the advantage of the new system is perhaps less revolutionary than might sometimes be suggested in the rhetoric surrounding the system's introduction.

Parallel systems

Very brief mention is needed of the existence of parallel systems of control in the management of the built and natural environment. When working through the process of development, it is important to be aware that planning is but one system in play. Alongside this, other key systems may also need to be considered. Key examples include:

- **Listed Building Consent (LBC) and Scheduled Ancient Monument Consent (AMC):** These systems exist to allow for additional controls and protections of heritage buildings (through LBC) and structures/monuments (LBC or AMC). As application and decision-making systems, they are comparable to the planning system and dealt with in much the same way (and typically by some of the same people), but designated assets (which are 'Listed', or 'Scheduled') are more tightly controlled; indeed, any changes to these buildings beyond like-for-like repairs typically need consent. This means that changes to such protected assets that do not require planning permission may well still require separate LBC/AMC. Applications for consent through these systems only cover the heritage implications of the proposal.

- **Advertisement Consent:** This is a bespoke system for controlling advertisements. Again, the system is unique but works on the same principle as planning permission. Advertising Consent is also comparable to the planning permission approach in that it also embraces the proportionality principle (see Table 6.2).

Table 6.2: Advertisement Consent approach comparison

Planning Permission	Advertisement Consent 'equivalent'
Not development	Excluded from consent
Permitted development	Deemed consent
Express planning permission	Express consent

Adam Sheppard (2018)

Advertising Consent is more limited (understandably) in its scope than planning permission, using only 'amenity' and 'public safety' as the basis for decisions. These works are quite broad in their scope, however, meaning that decisions can have due regard to a range of matters. The decision process is comparable in other respects too, with Special Areas of Control being used in the same way that planning generally uses area-based restrictions to limit permitted development rights.

- **Building regulations:** These are concerned with more structural matters, including building services, access (in line with the Equalities Act 2010), and health and safety. Being 'regulations', these constitute a very different approach to planning, because they are a set of regulations against which compliance is required – there is no discretion.

In addition to the three examples above, one must also be mindful of other systems, such as Licensing and Environmental Health, for instance, that will need to be considered, as well as other regulations which will need to be complied with, for example, health and safety. Add to this land and property law, and contracts, and we can see that the management of the built and natural environment is a web of systems that each have their own particular functions and which, hopefully, come together to provide comprehensive control.

Planning enforcement

All systems need to ensure that they are robust and not abused. For planning, a system of enforcement exists to ensure the planning process is adhered to. Enforcement is a specialist area of planning, but sits firmly within the planning family, ensuring change occurs appropriately. Enforcement teams, acting in response to monitoring acuities or information from communities or colleagues, can take action to ensure that unauthorised development is regularised and development undertaken through proper processes. Enforcement continues our proportionality narrative: the system does not exist to punish; it is intended to achieve successful outcomes. This may mean that a 'retrospective' planning application is the best option to securing planning permission for something which is otherwise unauthorised, or a 'notice' can be served to require compliance or undertake to resolve a given issue. Enforcement tries to be constructive in its approach, seeking a positive outcome. But it is also the case that enforcement teams have a range of options available to them to ensure the planning system is robust and complied with, including, for example, the ultimate option of court action and the associated fines or, in extreme circumstances, prison (Sheppard et al, 2017).

Conclusions

In this chapter we have explored and considered the planning decision-making space, and the processes and systems which exist to operationalise planning. Plans and policies create our direction of travel, but we need a system in place to enable the vision to be delivered appropriately and effectively. The development management aspects of planning are critical; they are how we control and manage change, ensuring its acceptability and, hopefully, successful delivery.

Further reading

For a more detailed consideration of the matters discussed in this chapter, the following is recommended:

Sheppard, A., Peel, D., Richie, H. and Berry, S. (2017) *The essential guide to planning law: Decision-making and practice in the UK*, Bristol: Policy Press.

For further detailed consideration of the process of development and wider planning system and decision-making process, the following are recommended:

Cullingworth, B., Nadin, V., Hart, T., Davoudi, S., Pendlebury, J., Vigar, G., Webb, D. and Townshend, T. (2015) *Town and country planning in the UK* (15th edn), Abingdon, Oxon: Routledge.

Ratcliffe, J., Stubbs, M., Keeping, M. (2009) *Urban planning and real estate development* (3rd edn), London: Routledge.

You can also find more detail about the systems around the UK, including the details of permitted development rights and planning processes, via the following government websites, which provide current and comprehensive information:

England, Planning Portal (remembering to identify 'England' as your location): https://www.planningportal.gov.uk

Northern Ireland, Planning Portal: https://www.planningni.gov.uk

Scotland, ePlanning Scotland: https://eplanning.scotland.gov.uk/ WAM

Wales, Town Planning Portal (remembering to identify 'Wales' as your location): https://www.planningportal.gov.uk

Finally, if you would like a more legalistic discussion, the following are recommended:

Dowling, J. (1995) *Northern Ireland planning law*, Dublin: Gill and Macmillan.

Duxbury, R. (2012) *Telling and Duxbury's planning law and procedure* (15th edn), Oxford: Oxford University Press.

McMaster, R. Smith, G., Prior, A, and Watchman, J. (2013) *Scottish planning law*, London: Bloomsbury Publishing.

Moore, V. and Purdue, M. (2012) *A practical approach to planning law* (12th edn), Oxford: Oxford University Press.

Note

[1] A statutory undertaker is an organisation that has legal rights defined in law to undertake specified development and works to the highways. Typically these are utility companies and organisations like Network Rail.

7

Enabling planning and change

Introduction

This chapter is focused around the notion of planning as a constructive and positive instrument for society and development delivery, but also as an instrument working within the wider process of development, where barriers to implementation can be challenging and a change to governance and finance is sometimes required.

The chapter is broadly split into two sections. The first considers how, in parallel to the planning application system, the wider act and art of planning is undertaken with the support of 'planning gain' to facilitate and enable positive change. The second considers the fact that there sometimes needs to be a change in how the process of development operates, with areas such as governance, planning instruments and finance sometimes needing to be adapted to create deliverable and viable development.

Planning gain
Philosophy and concept

Planning gain comes in different forms, but it is essentially either a financial payment to deliver something, or the direct provision of that something. Planning gain is an important part of how planning systems manage the full impact of change. Systems vary, but the concept is common around the world. It is through planning gain that impacts of change can be comprehensively managed and the public interest ensured through the delivery of necessary and societally expected infrastructure.

It is important to remember that behind any development is usually a financial gain; the process of development not only enables positive change, it also ultimately results in something of greater worth emerging from a given site. Through the process of development, profits are achieved. It is the private sector that principally delivers development, and this is, of course, a profit-making operation in most cases. The private interest can therefore be generally accepted as being a profit-making stakeholder within the process of development; even a house extension will normally increase the value of a home. Planning does not 'object' philosophically to this profit being made; we live in a free-market, broadly capitalist society, after all. But, it is also the case that alongside this profit come impacts. Impacts will often be good: a redevelopment will hopefully be contributing to the economy, character and appearance of the area, community opportunity, environmental gains and so forth. But impacts can also be challenging, placing extra demands upon social and physical infrastructure – more cars on the road, for example, and more people placing a demand on schools, libraries, public transport and so on. Planning gain is essentially how all of this is balanced; positive and challenging impacts occur, but whereas positive impacts benefit the developer and society, challenging impacts must be offset by the state (typically the local authority) in a context where profit is being made by someone else. It is therefore considered only 'fair' that some of this profit is effectively put back into society to help mitigate the challenges arising. The philosophy of planning gain is therefore a closing of the loop in the process of development: society facilitates and is impacted upon by development that has achieved gains, including profit; planning gain ensures some of this financial gain is fed back into society (Greed, 1996).

The concepts underpinning planning – the balancing of public and private interests, and the need to deliver sustainable development – are at the fore when it comes to planning gain. Planning attempts to manage change in the built and natural environment, and much of this occurs through the plans made, protections put in place and the decisions taken to bring about new development. But to genuinely and comprehensively manage private sector-led development change, the state needs support to manage the resultant impacts, ensuring that we have the road capacity, schools, libraries, health and emergency services, and so on, that we all expect and need.

Historically, around the UK there has, over the last few decades, been a single approach to planning gain: the planning agreement.

Planning agreements/obligations

Around the UK a common approach is a legal agreement called a planning agreement or obligation. This is an agreement which the applicant partners and the local authority sign up to, enabling the planning gain to legally and practically occur. It will specify precise financial payments to be made to the local planning authority to support them to deliver required physical and social infrastructure, and/or it will specific works and provisions the developers agree to deliver themselves. This will be a negotiated agreement which runs alongside, and is linked to, the impacts/implications of, a specific planning application. The agreement will lead to the developers delivering, or giving money to the local authority to deliver, the planning gain considered necessary and appropriate in relation to the approved development scheme. The main difference between a planning agreement and an obligation is that an agreement is negotiated by both parties, whereas an obligation is proposed to the local authority by the development party.

A planning agreement/obligation will exist alongside a planning permission. The amount to be paid is negotiated, but it is derived from an evidence base. From the local authority perspective, amounts are established based on the cost implications of new development. This will often be modelled on a formula, for example, £x per bedroom created or square metres of development proposed. These costs will be impact-based, so should be set at a level where the monies will allow for the 'need' to be addressed, whether that is building or upgrading a road junction, new school facilities, or a contribution towards an increased use of the library/community facilities/social support services. Planning agreements/obligations are also an important means by which to deliver affordable housing: typically, planning policy will require a certain percentage of housing schemes over a set size to be 'affordable housing'. Planning gain is the mechanism that allows this to be delivered.

From the developer perspective, viability is key: to be deliverable, a scheme must be viable and desirable; if the planning gain costs are too high, they can make a scheme undeliverable. The developer will therefore work out how much they can afford to pay, allowing for development costs and a profit margin. This is a key element within the negotiation that will take place between the developer and the local planning authority; ultimately a compromise must be reached which delivers what is needed but retains viability for the scheme (Sheppard et al, 2017).

As you might expect, planning agreements/obligations can sometimes be controversial. There are different reasons for this, but the process and outcomes are central. For communities, planning agreements/obligations can bring great benefits, but people can feel excluded from the process and perhaps be unhappy with the outcome – for example, perhaps the affordable housing numbers end up lower than would be hoped for. For developers, the greatest challenge is arguably the uncertainty of planning agreements. Developers need to know development costs, but negotiations around planning agreements means these costs are variable and as such effectively unknown – a real challenge when planning a project. Despite these challenges, planning agreements/obligations are crucial to delivering planning gain and continue to be the principle mechanism in the UK.

Community Infrastructure Levy

In England and Wales (but not Scotland or Northern Ireland) a second system of planning gain also exists. This is called the Community Infrastructure Levy (CIL). This is a fixed levy/payment system which requires a developer to pay into a local authority funding pot, based on the type and amount of development proposed, to allow infrastructure to be delivered. A key difference between the legal agreement approach noted above and CIL is that CIL is not negotiable; it is an area-based fixed fee that must be paid. The charged amount is based on a simple equation:

Development amount × *levy rate* × *inflation measure* = *chargeable amount*

The levy rate itself is based upon a balance between an amount derived from the actual anticipated infrastructure costs established by the local authority's infrastructure plan (minus the monies received from other sources), tempered by a need for viability in the area to be assured. The CIL is therefore closing the funding gap between other local government income and expected infrastructure, while seeking to ensure that deliverability is not compromised (Sheppard et al, 2017).

In England and Wales this system sits alongside the planning agreement/obligation system, with the two models having different purposes: planning agreements/obligations are used to deliver on-site planning gain and affordable housing; CIL is spent off site anywhere in the local authority area to deliver social and/or physical infrastructure in line with an approved CIL list of 'needs'.

A key difference with CIL is that it can be used in a strategic way by the local authority to fund infrastructure. It is not directly tied to the individual development; rather, it supports the wider demands of that area. The introduction of CIL has been quite controversial in some respects; it could be seen as an additional cost or an inflexible approach, and one which may lack impact for a development which contributes to it. It has key advantages over planning agreements/ obligations for the development industry, however, because it is a known and certain cost, which aids development finance modelling and certainty; and for local authorities, it allows them to deliver their Local Plan comprehensively with the support of the monies received through the CIL (Sheppard, 2017).

Overcoming challenges

In this section there will be a consideration of how interventions into the free market are used to enable development and overcome barriers to implementation. It will consider spatially applied tools, such as Urban Development Corporations; Urban Regeneration Companies; and more localised approaches which involve changes to government, governance, power distribution and development approaches. Models which are focused more upon financial barriers will also be considered, specifically, Tax Increment Financing and Business Improvement Districts. Finally, Enterprise Zones will also be briefly considered in the context of implementation and delivery. There are too many mechanisms to present them all here, so this chapter presents a selection that represent different models of approach and which are currently in use/have particular value. These are intended to give an overview, so each will only be briefly introduced.

Barriers to implementation

Planning is taking place in a dynamic and challenging context. When considering the world in which planning occurs, it is clear that there are multiple factors that can make development delivery problematic. The development process depends upon the crucial need for a scheme to be viable and deliverable. This can be difficult for a range of reasons, which can conspire to make a scheme undeliverable, for example, if market conditions do not make a scheme financially viable. The key perspective we are thinking about here is how plans and policy can be impeded so that change does not happen or happens in a flawed or compromised way. Planning broadly works on the basis of public plans and policy creating a vision and framework for the future, which is then realised in partnership with the development industry through (primarily) private sector delivery. The state plans; the market provides. But what happens when this doesn't occur, or when it doesn't occur as we might have anticipated?

We can understand how planning implementation barriers might manifest themselves by drawing upon public policy (rather than planning-specific) theory from Peter Dorey (2014) in his book *Policy Making in Britain: An introduction*. This arranges the different forms of barriers which can present themselves into eight types. We have added a ninth to this list (see Box 7.1) to reflect the manner in which planning 'law' can disrupt implementation. This could sit within other barriers to varying degrees, but it is helpful to highlight it separately for the purposes of this book.

Box 7.1: Barriers to (planning) implementation

1. **External agencies or events impact upon delivery:** Policies/ actions of other organisations, or events, such as the performance of the economy, get in the way. A good example of this would be an economic condition which means that the private sector would see a development proposal as undesirable and would choose not to bring it forward.

2. **There are too many dependency relationships:** To deliver the policy as intended requires the agreement or cooperation of other actors. This can lead to communication problems or different organisations/individuals pursuing their own particular goals. Planning is a good example of an industry where multiple actors are involved and dependent upon each other. Where disconnects exist, delivery challenges can occur.

3. **There are too many decision points:** Once a policy is adopted there are too many stages in the delivery chain. Planning has a decision-making process that involves planning officers and managers, and committees, with the decision further influenced by other government agencies and stakeholders. In parallel, further permissions may be required from parallel systems of control with other decision makers. This creates a web of decision makers and influences, each of which could prove to be a barrier.

4. **Resources are inadequate:**

   a) There is insufficient time to achieve the aims/objectives of the policy.
   b) There are inadequate human resources – lack of staff or lack or suitably qualified personnel.
   c) There are inadequate financial resources – lack of finance or funding.

   These are all challenges that can present themselves within planning, with a system that is timed and demanding of resources, and dependent upon favourable financial conditions for implementation.

5. **The policy is based on an invalid theory of cause and effect:** Most policy is a response to a problem/situation, but are the policy makers' assumptions about the underlying causes of a particular problem correct? Will a given planning policy, plan or strategy resolve the problem? Or is it based on flawed understanding/interpretation?

6. **The objectives are unclear, incoherent and inconsistent:** It is important for objectives to be understood, clear and consistent with each other if we are to make sense of them and deliver on their requirements. Where this is not the case it becomes possible for incorrect or flawed implementation to take place, or indeed for implementation to fail altogether.

7. **The objectives are not understood or accepted by those who implement the policy:** Implementers may not fully understand the intent of the policy makers, or they may have different values or organisational goals. Is planning policy clear and applied consistently? This will always be difficult in a discretionary planning system where policy must be interpreted.

8. **Those to whom a policy is applied or targeted do not respond in the anticipated manner:** Will the majority of people accept the measures concerned and act accordingly? Does the plan

deliver what people want? If not, resistance can occur and objections may result.

9. **The specific regulatory framework associated with the delivery of policy is not effective and leads to unintended consequences:** An example we can arguably consider here might be the limitations of the Use Classes Order or permitted development rights/prior approval to allow for effective implementation of policy concerning housing or delivery of health outcomes.

Adapted by Sheppard from Dorey (2014).

Dorey talks about the idea of 'perfect implementation' but makes it clear that it is impossible to achieve this. The nature of our world is such that we can never remove barriers to implementation entirely; indeed, some are outside of our control (a global economic crash, for example). What we can do, though, is ensure we have an awareness of the potential for implementation barriers to arise and embrace this within our planning process to minimise their risk (adapted from Dorey, 2014).

Creating an environment where planning barriers are minimised involves ensuring that the 'mainstream' system is as effective and successful as possible. Sometimes, however, this is not enough, and further steps are needed to create a space where development can and will come forward. Historically around the UK, a range of initiatives – in particular, national initiatives – have been used. It goes beyond the scope of this book to present these, but an awareness of implementation barriers as an ongoing challenge is important; different models of governance, planning, finance and physical regeneration approaches have been operationalised, including large-scale interventionist regeneration schemes, focused, in particular, around a government response to post-industrial decline in the UK. In the further reading section at the end of this chapter you will find reference to publications that offer a comprehensive exploration of current and historical urban regeneration initiatives in the UK.

In the rest of this chapter we will very briefly present some ways in which changes can be made to the 'mainstream' process of development to create an environment where identified barriers to implementation can be overcome.

Finance

Given the focus of this book, we will be concentrating on area-based responses which embrace or link planning to some extent and seek to enable positive change in specific areas. In addition to the selected sample of area-based responses in this book, though, it is important to highlight that the financing of the development process is sometimes the critical challenge and as a result funding can occur through a diversity of financial models which go beyond the scope of this text. These can vary from grant funding to loan funding; they can be provided publicly or privately (or in combination); and can be available for different forms of development by type, scale and location. All of these are important to overcoming the key implementation challenge of difficult financial circumstances which may make a given site or area less attractive and viable/deliverable for the market.

Compulsory purchase

One very specific tool which also merits mention before we move on is the compulsory purchase order (CPO). One key challenge in moving development forward is complex land ownership, which can make it difficult to acquire land for new development. Indeed, sometimes resistance to land assembly can occur. Systems to compulsorily purchase land, or undertake expropriation as it is sometimes known, exist around the world in different forms. In the UK the approach to this is known as compulsory purchase. The process of development in the UK operates on a principle of market delivery, and for land assembly this should translate into the delivery of the required land through purchase and development. Sometimes, however, the market cannot deliver because a land owner may be unwilling to engage with the market and support delivery in the desired way. When this occurs, it is possible for an acquiring authority (typically the local authority) to force the sale of the property through a CPO. It can be a complex, lengthy and financially difficult process to have a CPO approved and enacted, but of course we are considering an extreme act of state intervention here: land being purchased without the willing consent of the landowner (Sheppard et al, 2017).

It must be stressed that compulsory purchase is only carried out in a scenario where it is absolutely necessary. This necessity must be grounded in the 'public interest', with the overriding value of the project (economic, social or environmental) outweighing the implications of the act of compulsory purchase. A CPO is therefore a challenging concept, and can be controversial, but sometimes it is used to ensure that land can be brought together and made available for comprehensive development. The failure to make the land available would represent a critical point of failure in the process of development and a very real barrier to implementation (Sheppard et al, 2017).

The remaining section of this chapter will make reference to CPO in some instances. It is a tool that has importance in complex regeneration projects and development proposals.

Area-based responses

When thinking about barriers to implementation, we can identify the fact that they will sometimes present themselves in specific geographical areas. Typically, this would be where a given area is particularly challenged by the local economic conditions and/or the complexity of the development demands. This will often be a regeneration scenario where the costs of the development and the complexity of, for example, land ownership, make it very difficult for the market to bring a scheme forward. Alternatively, it may be a broader intent to create a more favourable environment to encourage investment. The approaches discussed below are examples of various forms of area-based responses.

Urban Development Corporations

Urban Development Corporations (UDCs) are arguably the most 'extreme' form of delivery vehicle, and they represent a more extensive degree of state intervention. A UDC is a defined area within which the very governance of place is changed: instead of the local authority, a statutory body is created and put in place to oversee the regeneration of the area. UDCs are typically created for large areas of land requiring comprehensive regeneration in challenging circumstances. Classic examples would be the Isle of Dogs in London (now Docklands) or 'Tiger Bay' (now Cardiff Bay). These are large areas that had suffered extreme decline and presented such financial and complexity challenges that a traditional planning response would arguably not have delivered the desired change. Often facing challenges around complex land ownership, contamination and an unattractive economic development environment, the UDC represents a powerful response (Tallon, 2013).

A UDC is a body which has complete power and control over an area. It is managed by an appointed board which is principally business-led. The local authority becomes a consultee for changes in this specific area, but otherwise effectively loses control and influence over this space (though activities of the UDC should be aligned to the local authority aspirations). Because the UDC represents a new body, it is sometimes referred to as a 'delivery vehicle'. A UDC will be time-limited (15/20 years) and will benefit from considerable government funding. It will also have considerable planning powers, including direct powers to produce and adopt plans, to make decisions through development management, and to pursue compulsory purchase. Internal organisational arrangements ensure integrity, but what is created is nevertheless an unelected body with the power to create a plan, make decisions against that plan and undertake compulsory purchase if required. This can be a controversial arrangement for reasons around democratic accountability and the extent to which the UDC balances economic regeneration with wider social and environmental considerations, but UDCs bring money and the ability to deliver major regeneration schemes in a time-sensitive manner (Tallon, 2013).

By visiting places such as London Docklands and Cardiff Bay, it is very easy to see the positive changes that have taken place. The approach to delivering these developments, however, as well as the criticisms they sometimes face from a community and environmental perspective, have made them unpopular with some people. The introduction of an urban development corporation in central Bristol in 1989, for example, was particularly known for being a challenging UDC (see Tallon, 2013). Despite this, UDCs are still used to deliver large-scale and complex developments, and a counter-critic might argue that, while controversial in some respects, they deliver results in circumstances where other measures and forms of delivery vehicle might not (Tallon, 2013).

Urban Regeneration Companies

An Urban Regeneration Company (URC) has some comparisons to a UDC, but it represents a different approach to the same concept. Whereas a UDC will take power and control to deliver results, a URC instead brings together the people that have the power and control to work in partnership to bring about the desired change.

URCs are non-statutory multi-agency partnerships, which means that as an entity they have no direct powers, but through the stakeholders (in particular, local authorities, and the former regional funding and governance bodies) are able to draw on their own competencies and deliver the desired impacts. URCs will commission master plans and development briefs from industry partners, draw on the local authority compulsory purchase powers, make planning decisions through the local planning authority, and draw on funding from a range of public and private sector sources. As with UDCs, URCs are time-limited and typically focused on delivering large-scale regeneration projects in complex and challenging circumstances (Tallon, 2013).

The URC model is less controversial than the UDC model for some, because it embraces partnership and a participative approach.

The board will have a balanced membership drawn from the public, private and third sectors, and it is through existing and established bodies that decisions are made and actions undertaken. This means they can be seen as more democratically accountable, particularly through the key role played by the local authority, and also, perhaps, more balanced in their objectives around economic, social and environmental change. URCs can, through their partnerships, bring about comprehensive redevelopment projects and overcome challenges around, for example, complex land ownership and difficult financial circumstances. They also create an organisational approach which is positive and effective, focusing upon the successful delivery of the area project (Tallon, 2013).

Looking around the UK at cities such as Gloucester, with its regenerated docks, it is easy to see both the successes of and the challenges faced by the URC model. URCs have delivered significant change, but they were also impacted upon by the changes to government and governance introduced by the Coalition government of 2010. Following their election success, the Coalition scrapped the Regional Assemblies (regional government) and Regional Development Agencies (regional funding bodies). The result of this was that URCs lost significant funding. Without this important public money, and in a wider context where private sector cash and local authority monies were limited, most activities ground to a halt and the URCs 'wound up'. Areas like Gloucester Docks continue to regenerate, but the rate of change in the absence of the URC has likely been much slower.

Local initiatives

A local initiative is essentially a bespoke local response to the demands of the circumstances. Conceptually, they are similar to URCs, working on the principle of the 'sum of their parts' bringing the necessary powers and influence required. Whereas the URC programme was a national strategy, the local initiative is more of a 'bottom-up' response. Local initiatives can take many different forms, but they will typically be a partnership between the local authority and third/private sector organisations plus, perhaps, regional organisations such as the former Regional Development Agencies.

Local initiatives can vary from being single sites to large-scale regeneration projects. The aim, though, remains the same: to overcome implementation and delivery challenges. This could range from 'pump priming' a site (making it ready for development) through dealing with contamination, access or infrastructure issues, to resolving land ownership challenges, master planning, project management or securing financing. The result of these efforts is a more favourable environment in which development can take place, with the private sector/market seeing the area as more attractive/ viable/deliverable.

As with a URC, the local initiative's strength lies in its ability to overcome land ownership, financial and organisational/scale complexity challenges. Also as with URCs, they face challenges around funding, which, particularly following the scrapping of the Regional Development Agencies, now demands significant investment from local authorities and the private sector, something which can be difficult to achieve in some circumstances. A visit to an area which has seen a local initiative in operation at a larger scale, such as Hereford, provides evidence of their impacts and the challenges they face; key projects are evident, but so too are the areas that are taking longer to come forward for (re)development than was hoped, as a result of ongoing implementation barriers, in particular, an unfavourable financial environment and scale complexity challenges.

Business Improvement Districts

Business Improvement Districts (BIDs), as with other instruments such as Enterprise Zones and Tax Increment Financing (see below), were first seen in the United States. BIDs are now well established in the UK, having been enabled by legislation in the early 2000s. They are an area-based approach and represent something that in some respects is really quite innovative: the private sector delivering public goods.

Although BIDs vary in size, location and purpose, they are underpinned by a common approach. In a BID businesses work in partnership with the local authority within a defined geographical area. Within this space the local authority essentially supports local businesses to pay more tax and to capture this additional income for reinvestment into the area in question. The decision to pursue a BID is taken on the basis of a vote (by owners and tenants), with a majority required for the BID to be introduced (Cook, 2008).

Where a BID is introduced, it is operated on a not-for-profit basis, with a mandatory levy on all defined rate payers (via business rates). This additional levy is captured by the local authority and given to the BID to invest in itself. A BID will have a fixed five-year life cycle, at the end of which a further vote is held and a decision taken on whether to run the BID for a further five years, and so on. The local authority therefore acts to facilitate the BID, but it is the private sector that funds it and makes decisions on how the additional funding should be secured (Cook, 2008).

BIDs are often found in city centre locations where retailers find advantage in using BID funding to support events, security/ maintenance/cleaning teams, street furniture, flowerbeds, signage, street/road surfacing improvements, free WiFi, advertising and such like. The logic is clear: by creating a more attractive environment, more people will come to the area and spend money in the local shops, cafes, bars and so on. It creates an upwards cycle of improvement.

The ongoing existence of BIDs suggests that they are generally well received and valued as an area-based response. They overcome the barriers of limited local authority resources, in particular, enabling positive and constructive improvements to be made in scenarios where otherwise this might not have been possible due to public sector limitations.

Tax Increment Financing

Tax Increment Financing (TIF) is a model that has been embraced in the UK relatively recently, despite being in use in the United States since the 1950s. TIF is essentially an area-based financial model based upon local government borrowing against their overall revenue stream. In the UK, it was operationalised following the election of the Coalition government. This was in a wider context wherein the government did away with a key form of organisation: Regional Development Agencies. The need for large-scale funding for development projects required new responses to ensure that the financial barrier to implementation did not develop in the vacuum created by the loss of this key funding source (Squires and Hutchison, 2014).

TIF works on the principle of local government borrowing money, which can then be repaid by drawing on an increased future income. The money borrowed by local government can be used to support redevelopment projects where barriers to implementation exist around finances. The delivery of this development will, through traditional local taxes such as business rates paid by the new occupiers of the scheme, then be used to pay off the borrowing. So the borrowing is repaid using future tax revenues from the redeveloped scheme (Squires and Hutchison, 2014).

Around the UK there are examples of TIFs being used in Edinburgh, London and Manchester. They are not widespread, the system is quite new, and they are not without criticism (will new opportunities be generated, or will relocation occur?) or indeed risk – for the local authority, in particular (which is dependent upon slightly unpredictable future income to repay the borrowing) – but they do offer an interesting new opportunity.

Enterprise Zones

Enterprise Zones are a well-established model in the UK. They are, simply put, the bringing together of two things: regulatory change and tax relief. The idea behind an Enterprise Zone is to create an environment that the market sees as more attractive, encouraging investment. The most common way to create this environment is through tax relief, which is offered to businesses that locate themselves within the designated area, and permitted development rights variations (through Local Development Orders – see Chapter

6). This creates a space where the costs of running a business are reduced, and it is easier to adapt and expand a building because greater permitted development rights are available (Tallon, 2013).

The Enterprise Zone model is particularly popular in business parks, industrial estates and large industrial/business sites; from the planning perspective, these will be less problematic because greater flexibility can be provided through permitted development rights with a reduced fear of undesirable (and particularly residential) impact. The impact of Enterprise Zones is much debated; although they can be seen as more attractive to businesses, they carry management costs for local authorities, who also lose revenue from planning applications that would otherwise be received. In some cases, there is also evidence of businesses relocating relatively locally to gain the advantages of the area, reducing their strategic value and creating challenges elsewhere in the local area (Tallon, 2013).

Conclusions

In this chapter we have considered two things: first, how can the wider act and art of planning be comprehensively operationalised? And second, what happens when the market does not provide for and help deliver our plans, policies and aspirations? Key to the matters considered in this chapter is the fact that much of the enabling activity we have looked at takes place *outside* the planning system; it is the wider context that is being reshaped to support planning and help to overcome barriers to implementation. It is easy to associate planning with the planning *system*. The planning system is how core planning activity occurs and is operationalised, but the wider act and art of planning is far broader in scope, and is linked to matters as diverse as land ownership, finance, and governance structures and approaches.

In this book we have taken a journey to develop an understanding of what planning is, and to explore its historical narrative, governance, application and delivery. But this book is only the tip of the iceberg, a first step into a fascinating area which touches on the lives of every single person in the UK in some way. Hopefully, you feel inspired to take this further now; if so, a good starting point is to review the further reading lists at the end of each chapter. Maybe study and/or a career in this field appeals?

Further reading

For further discussion concerning planning gain, the following provides a little more detail:

Sheppard, A., Peel, D., Richie, H. and Berry, S. (2017) *The essential guide to planning law: Decision-making and practice in the UK*, Bristol: Policy Press.

For a detailed consideration of planning gain, the following is recommended as a detailed and comprehensive read:

Crook, T., Henneberry, J. and Whitehead, C. (2016) *Planning gain: Providing infrastructure and affordable housing*, Chichester: Wiley.

For further detailed consideration of UK urban regeneration approaches, the following are both recommended as comprehensive and detailed guides which explore the historical narrative as well as current and key approaches:

Tallon, A. (2013) *Urban regeneration in the UK* (2nd edn), London: Routledge.
Jones, P. and Evans, J. (2013) *Urban regeneration in the UK: Boom, bust and recovery* (2nd edn), London: Sage.

References

Abercrombie, P. (1933) *Town and country planning*, London: Thornton Butterworth.

Aldridge, H. R. (1915) *The case for town planning*, London: National Housing and Town Planning Council.

APA (American Planning Association) (2018) *Great Places in America* [online], https://www.planning.org/greatplaces/

Arnstein, S. (1969) 'A ladder of citizen participation', *Journal of American Institute of Planners*, 35, July, 216–224.

Barton, H. (2016) *City of well-being: A radical guide to planning*, London: Routledge.

Beresford, M. (1967) *New towns of the Middle Ages: Town plantation in England, Wales and Gascony*, London: Lutterworth Press.

Biddle, M. and Hill, D. (1971) 'Late Saxon planned towns', *Antiquaries Journal*, 51: 76–8.

Booth, P. (2003) *Planning by consent: The origins and nature of British development control*, London: Routledge.

Brindley, T., Rydin, Y. and Stoker, G. (1996) *Remaking planning: The politics of urban change* (2nd edn), London: Routledge.

Brownhill, S. and Bradley, Q. (2017) *Localism and neighbourhood planning: Power to the people?*, Bristol: Policy Press.

Buckingham, J. S. (1849) *National evils and practical remedies*, London: Jackson, Fisher, Son and Co.

Burke, G. (1975) *Towns in the making*, London: Edward Arnold.

Business Insider (2013) '11 American cities that are shells of their former selves' [online], www.businessinsider.com/american-cities-in-decline-2013-6?IR=T

Claydon, J. (1999) 'Negotiations in planning', in C. Greed (ed) *Implementing town planning: The role of town planning in the development process*, Harlow: Essex: Longman Group Ltd, pp 110–20.

Claydon, J. and Chick, M. (2005) 'Teaching negotiations', *Planning Practice and Research*, 20(2), 221–34.

Cook, I. (2008) 'Mobilising urban policies: the policy transfer of US Business Improvement Districts to England and Wales', *Urban Studies*, 45(4): 773–95.

Coulson, A. (2003) 'Land-use planning and community influence: a study of Selly Oak, Birmingham', *Planning, Practice and Research*, 18(2-3): 179–95.

Cullingworth, B. and Nadin, V. (2006) *Town and country planning in the UK* (14th edn), Abingdon, Oxon: Routledge.

Cullingworth, B., Nadin, V., Hart, T., Davoudi, S., Pendlebury, J., Vigar, G., Webb, D. and Townshend, T. (2015) *Town and country planning in the UK* (15th edn), Abingdon, Oxon: Routledge.

Curry, N. (2012) 'Community participation in spatial planning: exploring relationships between professional and lay stakeholders', *Local Government Studies*, 38(3): 345–66.

Damer, S. and Hague, C. (1971) 'Public participation in planning: a review', *Town Planning Review*, 42(3): 217–32.

Davidoff, P. (1965) 'Advocacy and pluralism in planning', *Journal of the American Institute of Planners*, 31(4): 331–8.

Davidson S. (1998) 'Spinning the wheel of participation', *Planning*, 1262: 14–15.

DCLG (Department of Communities and Local Government) (2012) *National Planning Policy Framework: Consultation proposals*, London: DCLG.

Dennis, N. (1972) *Public participation and planners' blight*, London: Faber and Faber.

Department for Infrastructure (2012) *Regional Development Strategy 2035*, Belfast: DfI Planning.

Department for Infrastructure (2015) *Strategic Planning Policy Statement*, Belfast: DfI Planning.

Department of the Environment (1997) *Planning obligations*, Circular 1/97, London: Department of the Environment.

Dobry, G. (1975) *The Dobry Report: Review of development control; branch input into relaxation of development controls*, London: HMSO

Dorey, P. (2014) *Policy making in Britain: An introduction*, London: Sage Publications.

DTLR (Department of Transport, Local Government and the Regions) (2001) *Planning: Delivering a fundamental change*, Green Paper, London: DTLR.

Financial Times (2017) 'Shrinking cities: population decline in the world's rust-belt areas' [online], https://www.ft.com/content/d7b00030-4abe-11e7-919a-1e14ce4af89b

Greater London Authority (GLA) (2017) *London Plan annual monitoring report 2015/16*, London: GLA.

Greed, C (ed) (1996) *Implementing town planning*, Harlow: Longman.

Greed, C. and Johnson, D. (2014) *Planning in the UK: An introduction*, London: Palgrave Macmillan.

Hall, P. and Tewdwr-Jones, M. (2010) *Urban and regional planning* (5th edn), London: Routledge.

Haughton, G and Allmendinger, P. (2011) 'Moving on – from spatial planning to localism and beyond', *Town and Country Planning Association*, April, 80(4): 184–7.

Haughton, G. and Allmendinger, P. (2012) 'Spatial planning and the new localism', *Planning Practice and Research*, 28(1): 1–5.

Healey, P. (1997) *Collaborative planning: Shaping places in fragmented societies*, Vancouver: UBC Press.

Hindle, P. (2002) *Medieval town plans*, Buckinghamshire: Shire Publications.

Howard, E. (1898) *To-morrow: A peaceful path to real reform*, London: Swan Sonnenschein.

Intergovernmental Panel on Climate Change (IPCC) (2014) *Fifth assessment report* [online], www.ipcc.ch

Jackson, J.N. (1964) 'Planning education and the public', *Journal of the Town Planning Institute*, 50 (6): 231–7.

JCS (2017) *Gloucester, Cheltenham and Tewkesbury Joint Core Strategy 2011–2031* (adopted December 2017), Cheltenham: JCS.

Karakiewicz, J., Yue, A. and Paladino, A. (2015) *Promoting sustainable living: Sustainability as an object of desire*, Abingdon, Oxon: Routledge.

Lawrence, A. (2006) '"No personal motive?" Volunteers, biodiversity, and the false dichotomies of participation', *Ethics, Place and Environment*, 9(3): 279–98.

Lichfields (2018) *Local choices? Housing delivery through neighbourhood plans*, London: Nathaniel Lichfield and Partners Limited.

Lilley, K., Lloyd, C. and Trick, S. (2005) 'Mapping the medieval townscape: a digital atlas of the new towns of Edward I', York: Archaeology Data Service, http://archaeologydataservice.ac.uk/archives/view/atlas_ahrb_2005/index.cfm

Lovering, J. (1995) 'Creating discourses rather than jobs: the crisis in the cities and the transition fantasies of intellectuals and policy makers', in P. Healey, S. Cameron, S. Davoudi, S. Graham and A. Madani-Pour (eds) *Managing cities: The new urban context*, Chichester: John Wiley and Sons, pp 109–26.

McAuslan, P. (1980) *The ideologies of planning law*, Oxford: Pergamon Press.

MHCLG (Ministry of Housing, Communities and Local Government) (2018) *National Planning Policy Framework*, London: MHCLG.

Michener, V. J. (1998) 'The participatory approach: contradiction and co-option in Burkina Faso', *World Development*, 26(12): 2105–18.

Nadin, V. and Seaton K. (2006) 'The idea of policy integration and spatial planning', briefing note for DCLG *Spatial Plans in Practice* research project, University of the West of England, unpublished.

Nolan Committee (1997) *The third report of the Committee on Standards in Public Life* (Cm 3702-1), London: HMSO.

Office for National Statistics (2018) 'Population estimates' [online], https://www.ons.gov.uk/peoplepopulationandcommunity/populationandmigration/populationestimates

PAG (Planning Advisory Group) (1965) *The future of development plans: Report of the Planning Advisory Group*, Ministry of Housing and Local Government, London: HMSO.

Petrie, F. (2013) *Illahun, Kahun and Gurob*, Cambridge: Cambridge University Press.

Planning Aid (undated) 'How to resource your neighbourhood plan' [online], https://www.ourneighbourhoodplanning.org.uk/storage/resources/documents/How_to_resource_your_neighbourhood_plan4.pdf

Platt, C. (1976) *The English medieval town*, London: Secker and Warburg.

Poxon, J. (2000) 'Solving the development plan puzzle in Britain: learning lessons from history', *Planning Perspectives*, 15(1): 73–89.

Quality Assurance Agency for Higher Education (QAA) (2016) *Subject benchmark statement for town and country planning*, Gloucester: QAA.

Ratcliffe, J., Stubbs, M. and Keeping, M. (2009) *Urban planning and real estate development* (3rd edn), London: Routledge.

RTPI (Royal Town Planning Institute) (2005) *Guidelines on effective community involvement and consultation: RTPI Good Practice Note 1*, London: RTPI.

RTPI (2012) *Policy Statement on Initial Planning Education*, London: RTPI.

RTPI (2018) 'About the RTPI' [online], www.rtpi.org.uk/about-the-rtpi/

RTPI and PAS (Planning Advisory Service) (2013) *The National Competency Framework for Planners*, London: RTPI and PAS.

Rydin, Y. (1993) *The British planning system: An introduction*, Basingstoke: Macmillan.

Rydin, Y. (1999) 'Public participation in planning', in B. Cullingworth (ed) *British planning: 50 years of urban and regional policy*, London: Athlone Press, pp 184–197.

Scottish Government (2014a) *National Planning Framework 3*, Edinburgh: Scottish Government.

Scottish Government (2014b) *Scottish Planning Policy*, Edinburgh: Scottish Government.

Sharp, T. (1938) *English panorama*, Colchester and London: Spottiswoode Ballantyne and Co.

Shaw, K. and Robinson, F. (2010) 'UK urban regeneration policies in the early twenty-first century: continuity or change?', *Town Planning Review*, 81(2): 123–49.

Sheppard, A., Burgess, S. and Croft, N. (2015) 'Information is power: public disclosure of information in the planning decision-making process', *Planning Practice and Research*, 30(4): 443–56.

Sheppard, A., Peel, D., Richie, H. and Berry, S. (2017) *The essential guide to planning law: Decision-making and practice in the UK*, Bristol: Policy Press.

Sitte, C. (1889) *City planning according to artistic principles*, published in 1965 by Phaidon Press.

Skeffington, A. (1969) *People and planning: Report of the Committee on Public Participation in Planning*, London: HMSO.

Squires, G. and Hutchison, N. (2014) 'The death and life of Tax Increment Financing (TIF): redevelopment lessons in affordable housing and implementation', *Property Management*, 32(5): 368–77.

Tallon, A. (2013) *Urban regeneration in the UK* (2nd edn), London: Routledge.

TCPA (Town and Country Planning Association) (2017) 'Background Paper 2: The rise and fall of town planning' [online], https://www.tcpa.org.uk/Handlers/Download.ashx?IDMF=fffe8fd5-734f-489d-bd9e-d4e211a91b0b

TCPA (2018) 'Our history' [online], https://www.tcpa.org.uk/our-history-1

Triggs, H.I. (1911) *Town planning, past, present and possible*, London: Methuen and Co.

Tritter, J.Q. and McCallum A. (2006) 'The snakes and ladders of user involvement: moving beyond Arnstein', *Health Policy*, 76: 156-168.

United Nations (2015) *Sustainable Development Goals* [online], https://www.un.org/sustainabledevelopment/sustainable-development-goals/

United Nations (2017) *World population prospects: The 2017 revision* [online], https://www.un.org/development/desa/publications/world-population-prospects-the-2017-revision.html

Valler, D., Phelps, N.A. and Wood, A.M. (2012) 'Planning for growth? The implications of localism for "Science Vale", Oxfordshire, UK', *Town Planning Review*, 83(4): 457–88.

Wannop, U. (1999) 'New Towns' in B. Cullingworth (ed) (1999) *British planning: 50 years of urban and regional policy,* New Jersey: The Athlone Press, pp 213–31.

Ward, S. (2004) *Planning and urban change* (2nd edn), London: SAGE Publications Ltd.

Wates, N. (2014) *The community planning handbook* (2nd edn), London: Routledge Earthscan.

Welsh Government (2008) *Wales Spatial Plan* (2nd edn), Cardiff: Welsh Government.

Welsh Government (2016) *Planning Policy Wales* (9th edn), Cardiff: Welsh Government.

WHO (World Health Organization) (2018a) 'Air pollution' [online], www.who.int/airpollution/en/

WHO (2018b) 'Obesity and overweight' [online], www.who.int/mediacentre/factsheets/fs311/en/

Wilson, W., Barton, C. and Smith, L. (2018) *Tackling the under-supply of housing in England*, London: Houses of Parliament.

Index

Note: Page numbers in *italic* refer to figures or tables.